Life

WITH

JAMES

*From a Chance Meeting To
a 33-Year Partnership*

O. L. CONNELLY

CONTENTS

Chapter 1

A CHANCE MEETING

When I graduated from college in 1980 with my teaching degree, it was difficult finding a position in a Twin Cities area school district because, at the time, they were laying off many teachers. I thought I could substitute teach until I secured a position. But after two years, I was still unsuccessful in achieving this goal. In the fall of 1982, one of my brothers was moving down to Texas with a friend from school to complete an apprenticeship to become an electrical lineman. I decided to go down and visit him and make sure he got settled into his new environment. But when I mentioned this trip to a friend, he suggested that I not stay with my brother because the town he was living in would not be pleasant to visit. He said it would be more enjoyable for me to stay with a college friend of his in Houston and visit my brother during the day.

While staying with his friend, I met some of his neighbors, one of whom was a teacher in HISD. When I told him about my job search, he recommended I apply in Houston while I was there because they were always hiring. I was skeptical because the school year had already begun, but I took his advice and went to the district office to ask about the application process. I completed all the tests and paperwork successfully.

I was told they would contact me if they found any interested schools that wanted to interview me.

I returned to Minneapolis and continued substitute teaching and waiting tables. After about three weeks, I received a call from HISD; they had a few schools interested in seeing me. I made interview appointments for the next week and returned to Houston. I was able to stay with my new friend again, which saved me a lot of expense. After I completed my first day of interviews, I returned to the district office. I was told I had an offer for a third-grade position from the first principal I'd met with and was asked if I was interested. This was the principal whose first question to me was, "When can you start?" Since it was mid-November, I said I would like to wait until after the Christmas holidays. He was hoping I could begin the next Monday. His second question was what my thoughts were on paddling. Being from Minnesota and a former camp counselor, I thought, what does teaching have to do with canoeing? I hesitated and asked what the district policy was. He said that corporal punishment was allowed. Then it clicked. Oh, paddling! I said that though we did not do that in Minnesota, I would support the district policy.

After waiting this long for the opportunity to teach, I accepted the position and returned home to prepare for my move to Houston after the Christmas holidays. I now had a small group of friends in Houston, so the transition to a new city was very smooth, and I quickly established my new day-to-day routines.

It was Friday night in Houston, and I'd finished another week of teaching at the elementary school in the 5th Ward. I also worked a few nights as a waiter in a restaurant in the Museum District. But now it was time to go out with my friends for some fun, which meant heading to Rascals ... a popular gay bar/cabaret/restaurant off Westheimer Road.

My group of about a dozen friends was gathered in our usual spot near the bar. I had a boyfriend at the time that I'd met in Houston, but he'd recently moved to LA. I planned to move there after the close of the school year, so I was not out to meet any new people. At some point during the evening, a friend came up to me and, after some friendly chitchat, pointed out a man across the room and asked if I knew him. I didn't know him. The friend said this man wanted to meet me and asked if I would join them for a drink.

Seeing no harm, I walked over and was introduced to James. We talked for quite a while and got along very well, but we didn't share a lot of personal information. It was getting late, and we decided it was time to go home. While we were walking out to our cars, James asked me if I wanted to come over and see his new townhouse. I declined, and as we got to our cars, he asked if we could see each other sometime the next week. We exchanged information, but I wasn't sure if there would be another meeting.

The following week James called and asked if we could get together for dinner. We agreed on a date, time, and place, and I met him at the restaurant. The ambiance was pleasant, and it was quiet enough for us to easily converse. I was surprised at how easy it was to talk to James, as I tend to be on the quiet side. I found out he was in the oil business and had been married and had three children. He'd come out about a decade earlier and had moved from West Texas to Houston to begin a new life. I knew he was quite a bit older than I was, but I didn't know exactly how much older; he laughed and said that he never dated anyone over thirty and that I'd just made the cutoff. I had to work the next morning, and it was getting late, so we left to go home. Again on the way to our cars, he asked if I wanted to see his new townhouse. I declined and said I needed to go home. He seemed a little surprised by my response but asked if we could get together again. We discussed a few dates for the following week and agreed to firm up a date later.

I was experiencing some relationship conflict at this time and wasn't sure what to do or where this was going. I had just spent spring break with my boyfriend in LA, and it wasn't the best of times. He was going through a rough patch with employment issues, and it was a little uncomfortable being there. This was unusual for us, and I was having second thoughts about moving to be with him. I was unsure of where our relationship was going. I had only been in Houston for a year, and I'd made some good friends and was enjoying my job. As for LA, I only knew my boyfriend, and though I had a teaching contract with LAISD, they would not confirm which school I would be working in or what part of the district I would be located in.

And then there was James. I could tell he was surprised when I declined his two invitations to his townhouse. What he didn't realize was that I followed a three-date rule when meeting new people. Nothing intimate would happen until after the third date. I preferred to take things slowly. I wasn't sure of his motives, nor did I know many details of his day-to-day life. Then there was the age difference. James was in his early fifties, and I was just approaching thirty. Would we have enough in common? Could this work out for us? I enjoyed his company, and we got along really well, and I decided to cautiously move forward and see where things might lead.

James and I continued seeing each other over the next few weekends, usually for dinner. As each evening together came to a close, James would again ask if I would like to stop by the house, and each time I would say no. After about a month of dating, James called, and we decided to meet at Rascals for dinner. We stayed to watch the cabaret show and had a wonderful time. On the way to our cars, James asked one more time if I would like to see his new townhouse. This time I said yes. So I followed him home and went inside to take the tour. We walked into a two-story foyer that had a beautiful curved staircase up to the second floor. There was a large kitchen and eating area to the left with an adjoining dining room, with the living room and library to the right. It was all beautifully decorated and filled with an amazing art collection. After a few drinks, we went up to the master suite for our first intimate encounter, and I spent the night. The next morning we went downstairs and made some breakfast. James told me that he always washed his cars after Saturday breakfast and asked me to join him. We went out to the driveway, and he opened the garage doors. He began backing out his cars, starting with the Rolls Royce, followed by the Cadillac sedan. Then came the Mustang convertible. At the end of the line was my little Toyota Tercel.

James gave me a brief tutorial on his car-washing rituals, as each car had a specific set of procedures. We started with the Rolls and moved down the line until hours later; we finished the Mustang. I rarely washed my car by hand, so I thought we were finished. But James quickly corrected me and said we needed to do my car as well. We got started on it, and at one point, I went into the house for something; when I came out, I was surprised to see James scrubbing the tires on my car. I had never done this on any car I ever owned and was so impressed that James would treat my car with as much care as he took with his cars. This special time together began an unexpected turn in our relationship. Later that day, we went for a run in Memorial Park, showered, and made plans for dinner. I ended up spending the rest of the weekend at his house.

This became our routine for the next few months. He would travel to Austin every Monday morning where he and a partner owned a bank and return to Houston on Thursday evening. This schedule worked well for me as I could teach during the week and work a few nights at the restaurant, leaving the weekend open to spending time with James. We would get together for dinner on Thursday, and then I would come back on Friday night and spend the weekend with him. Every once in a while, he would need to go out of town, and I would follow my old-usual weekend routine—Friday night at Rascals, Saturday night at Rich's, and Sunday afternoon Tea Dance at JR's, hanging out with my friends.

One Sunday morning, after spending the weekend at James', I went back to my house, which I shared with two roommates. One of the roommates, Randy, was home, and he asked me if we could have a talk. We sat at the table, and he said he'd noticed something very different about me. I normally was home every night, but lately, I was staying out on most weekends. What was going on? Had I met someone? I shared with him that I had, and he wanted to know if he knew this person and who was it. I said James' name, and he looked at me kind of strangely and said,

"Do you mean the James Armstrong?" I said I didn't know if he was the James, so he described him to me, and I said that yes, it was James. He seemed quite surprised and asked, "How is that possible? When you go out, you never talk to anybody outside of your immediate group, and you always come home at the end of the night. How did this happen?" I recapped the last few months—when we met and what we'd been doing together, and Randy seemed quite shocked. He asked me a lot of questions as he was trying to process this new information. He said it was a lot to take in but wished me well.

As the school year was soon coming to an end, I had to make a big decision. Should I go with the original plan and move to LA, or stay in Houston and give this new relationship a chance? I'd never been in a situation like this and had no relationship history to guide this decision. So I decided to do what any sensible good gay boy would do and made plans to go to Europe for three weeks to get a clearer perspective of what I needed to do. About five years earlier, I'd spent nine months working at an International YMCA camp in England. Afterward, I spent ten weeks traveling throughout Europe, visiting a number of staff and campers. Over the years, I'd kept in touch with some of those people, who frequently asked when I was going to return to Europe. This would be the perfect time to plan a trip.

After setting the travel dates, making airline arrangements, and acquiring a Eurail Pass, I created the itinerary. I shared my travel plans with about ten friends and received confirmation from all of them. I flew directly to London and visited a friend in the Winchester area. While there, we took a day trip to the International YMCA camp and visited with staff members who still worked there from the time I was employed. I then caught the ferry to Calais on the northern coast of France and continued on to Rennes to visit friends from camp who had since gotten married. Next was a visit to a friend who lived on Lake Maggiore in northern Italy and who did not speak English. Though he was about half my age, he had some older, English-speaking friends who liked to sail, play soccer, and ride scooters around town.

Austria was next on the list, and I spent time with two friends, one in Lienz and the other in Dornbirn. Both of these guys spoke English fluently and were very sports-minded. They enjoyed taking hikes in the beautiful mountains surrounding both of their towns.

I then headed to Germany and visited two more friends, one who lived near Stuttgart and the other in Hamburg. Though both of these guys were campers when we met and were quite a bit younger than I, they had each visited me for a month in the states, and we shared a lot of common interests. I stopped in Paris on my way back to London and visited a friend who had worked with me at the restaurant in Houston but was now attending cooking school in Paris. I only spent one night there. I then took the ferry back to England, where I spent a few days in London. The last stop before returning home was a long weekend in NYC to visit a hometown friend who had moved there.

It was during that visit in NYC that I decided to call my boyfriend in LA and James in Houston to see what their reactions would be. This would help me decide whether I should move to LA and which relationship would best meet my needs. It also helped that my NYC friend loved to offer relationship advice, so I could bounce my options off of her. I first called LA, and we had a pleasant conversation. He was doing better now that he had found a new job he enjoyed. But when I called James, his first question was, "When are you coming home?" I said I would be back on Monday, but he said, no, that I needed to be back by Sunday morning. When I asked why he said we had a pool party to attend; he also had plans for us to travel to Santa Barbara the next week, followed by a week in Aspen, as well as other trips and events throughout the rest of the summer.

To say I was surprised was an understatement. I was not prepared for what he was telling me. My friend and I kept busy over the next two days but had many conversations about my immediate future. I finally made the decision to go back to Houston and further develop my relationship with James. But that meant I had to get back early Sunday morning. My friend's family had a place in the Poconos, and a group of us went there on Saturday for a day trip. It happened that one of the couples with us lived near Newark airport, where I was departing from. I went back with them so I could easily catch an early flight to Houston. I let James know of my travel plans, and he said he would pick me up at the airport. Because I had been traveling by backpack the previous three weeks and had made these last-minute travel plans to return to Houston, I didn't have much choice about what I could wear home. Also, because of the early flight, I wasn't able to shower and was, to say the least, a bit disheveled.

Apparently, and I didn't learn this until many years later when James saw me standing in the arrival area at the airport, he looked at me and was not pleased with what he saw. He thought he was making a big mistake and almost decided to drive off. Thankfully, he reconsidered, and we went to his house so I could get cleaned up. We went to the pool party (hosted by the mutual friend who first introduced me to James at Rascals) as planned and had a wonderful time. Because of my appearance at the airport, James decided the next day that we needed to do some shopping for upcoming summer trips and events. We went directly to the Galleria and spent a few hours at Nieman Marcus, creating my new look for the summer.

Our first trip together was to his friend's home in Santa Barbara. This was the first friend of James' that I had met. Until that point, he had kind of isolated me from his social circle and focused on me and how we could strengthen our relationship. We spent the next four days shopping, going out to lunch and dinner in the surrounding area, and walking to the beach each day. Our next trip took us to James' townhome in Aspen for the Fourth of July week. What was unique about this trip was that we were taking the bank's private plane. This form of transportation was something I had only heard of but never dreamed I would experience. It was the beginning of what would turn out to be an amazing lifestyle for which I was not at all prepared. We had lunch and dinner in many of the local restaurants and at some of the most beautiful mountain homes of James' many friends. The multiple hikes in the mountains were one of the highlights of the trip. Sometimes it was just the two of us; other times, we went with a small group. A prepared lunch was often served on the trail. The Fourth of July festivities were a lot of fun, with a parade through the downtown area and beautiful fireworks that evening. Every once in a while, we would run into celebrities walking around town, and I met a lot of wonderful people I would see again in the near future. I had a hard time adjusting to such an incredible experience but enjoyed every moment of it.

The last trip of the summer was the White Party in LA over Labor Day weekend. I thought my Aspen experience was going to be hard to beat, but I was about to experience a whole new level of amazement with a weekend of parties like no other. James and I stayed with friends of his who lived in the valley and were key organizers for the weekend. The events varied from pool parties to lunches and cocktail parties throughout the LA area. Private homes and estates in Bel Air, Brentwood, and Beverly Hills were just a few of the places where we would gather. There was also a lunch party on the beach and a tour of the area where the Summer Olympics had just been held. The last evening was at a large estate with a beautiful home and gardens all lit up for the evening. The main area of entertainment was on an elevated tennis court near the main house where the bars, food, dance floor, and tables were set up. It was a magical evening. I was taken to heights of entertainment I had never experienced before. I would see the core group of people I met this weekend many more times over the next few years.

This was the best summer I had ever had and was something I never could have dreamed of or created on my own. But it was time to get back to my normal routine of beginning another school year, working a few nights at the restaurant, and spending time with James on the weekends. It was also the beginning of something I had never heard of before ... the Houston Social Season.

Chapter 2

THE SOCIAL SEASON

As the fall season was approaching, James began talking about some new experiences that I needed to get prepared for, which meant another shopping trip. We were about to enter Houston's Social Season, where James had a prominent presence. He was about to take me along for the ride.

We went to a number of shops over the next few weeks so I could get a couple of suits, a tuxedo, and shoes, all of which would help prepare me for the variety of social and formal events we would be attending over the next nine months. These included opening nights at the opera, ballet, various museums, and the symphony. We would attend receptions, dinners, garden parties, and galas on most weekends. Sometimes we would attend these by ourselves; other times, we would escort two women and go as a small group. When this was the case, a recurring problem for me was dancing. I could fake my way through most situations, but not dancing.

James' solution was for me to take dance lessons. We found a local dance studio, and I signed up for ballroom dance lessons focusing on the waltz, fox trot, cha-cha, and rumba. The last time I'd taken dance lessons was a P.E. class in middle school, so the first few lessons were a challenge.

But as the weeks went by, I became more comfortable and could tell I was improving. I even began to look forward to the next lesson. We would have recitals every so often to provide us with the experience of performing our routines in front of an audience. What I soon found out was that there was an opportunity to compete with dance studios in two other Texas cities twice a year. Participation involved buying packets of lessons where I would learn up to four routines composed of two solo routines with my instructor and two group competitions. My first competition was going to be in San Antonio. We invited two of my sisters to come down from Minnesota, and the four of us attended together. This was an all-day event with the dancers divided into three levels of experience. The champion in each group would be awarded a trophy. Though my instructor and I did well with our routines, I was not expecting anything since this was my first competition. At the awards ceremony that evening, when they got to my group level to award Best Male Newcomer, they announced my name. I was surprised and very pleased to be selected, and we agreed that it was all worth it. James had such a good time that weekend, that after we returned home, he decided he would start taking lessons. We both participated in the next competition, and this time James won a trophy. Though we enjoyed going to the dance studio and were pleased with our progress, after a couple of years, we felt we had accomplished our goals and ended our lessons.

Another new experience for me was traveling to some of James' other vacation homes. Along with the one in Aspen, he had condos in NYC and Ft. Lauderdale. James had the condo in NYC because he was on the board of the New York City Opera at the invitation of the new director, Beverly Sills. He would fly up almost every month to attend meetings. We would usually travel to NYC at the beginning of December to enjoy the holiday decorations and again in the spring or fall, mostly to shop and see Broadway shows. We would also go to museums, art galleries, and favorite restaurants. Every once in a while, we would get invited to a gala fund-raiser in a beautiful ballroom or dinner or reception in a private residence. I really enjoyed getting to see some of the beautiful homes and apartments throughout the city.

The first time I went to Ft. Lauderdale, it was for Christmas, and this trip was combined with a visit to Aspen for New Year's. This time we flew in the bank's private plane, loading it up with Christmas gifts and two sets of wardrobe—clothes for the beach and the other set for winter. It was a little embarrassing to have so much stuff loaded onto the plane for just the two of us, but it seemed common practice for James. The condo was beautiful, with views of the ocean on one side and the Intracoastal Waterway on the other side. Shortly after we arrived, I was in the bedroom when I heard James laughing out loud in the living room and went in to see what he was doing. He was listening to A Prairie Home Companion on the radio. I was surprised he was familiar with the show. I had grown up with it in Minnesota and had attended the show live several times. This turned out to be an unexpected connection between us, and we would listen to the weekly show many times over the years. We attended the show live in both Austin and NYC.

When we were preparing to leave Ft. Lauderdale for Aspen, James received a distressing call from his mother's caregiver, saying that she had fallen and was in the hospital. He decided we should fly directly to Ft. Worth to check up on her. The pilot was able to make the necessary flight changes, and we headed back to Texas.

His mother ended up having a hip fracture, so she would be in the hospital for a while before going home. I stayed with James until after New Year's but needed to fly home to Houston to return to work. There was a direct flight from Love Field to Hobby, and we booked a seat for me. When we arrived at the airport, we noticed there weren't many people around the departure gate. When I entered the plane and started walking through the cabin, I was quite surprised to see there weren't any other passengers. I asked one of the flight attendants what was going on and was informed they had a group of passengers in Houston waiting to return to Dallas. They needed to get the plane down there even though there were no other passengers flying to Houston. She said I could sit anywhere, and they prepared for takeoff. It was a short flight, and at one point, the four flight attendants ended up sitting around me to keep me company. I asked them if they had ever had an experience like this, with only one passenger. They all said this was a first for them. When we arrived in Houston, I departed the plane and went into the terminal, where the Dallas passengers were waiting to board. They noticed I was the only one getting off the plane and asked where the other passengers were. When I replied I was the only one, they kind of laughed at me as if I were joking. I said they could wait as long as they wanted, but I really was the only passenger. Then they looked at me again with wonder, trying to guess who I was and how I had secured a commercial jet just for me. This unique flight certainly made up for the missed experience to travel home on James' private plane, as previously planned.

There was, I learned, an alternate social season in Houston: the Gay Social Season. Up until then, I had not met many of James' gay friends and didn't realize how large of a group he was talking about until we began going to some of the parties and fund-raisers. A large group of these people, especially the older ones, mostly socialized by going out to dinner with friends or hosting cocktail or dinner parties in their homes. I didn't know many from this group. My gay lifestyle was going out with friends to the bars.

James decided to host a holiday party since he was settled into his new townhouse. I was surprised he wanted it to be formal and would require guests to wear tuxedos. I had never been to a holiday party this formal and became interested as James and his assistant began making the arrangements to include a caterer, florist, formal invitations, security, and valet parking. On the evening of the party, after I was finished getting dressed, I came down the staircase and was stopped in my tracks. I was caught off guard by a large group of waiters in white coats and gloves standing in two lines facing my direction at the bottom of the stairs, receiving last-minute instructions for the evening. I walked around the house and looked at all of the beautiful flowers and decorations in each room and found James in the library waiting for the first guests to arrive. It turned out to be a lovely party with over two hundred guests, and it lasted for hours. This would be the first of many parties James and I would host over our years together.

One night we were leaving for a black-tie event for a mostly gay group to benefit a local charity. James had purchased one of the major tables, and we had eight guests join us in the ballroom of a downtown hotel. Before we left, James surprised me with a gift of beautiful onyx and diamond studs and cuff links. This would be the first of many pieces of jewelry I would receive from the James collection of fine jewelry. It was a beautiful event with amazing decorations, a great orchestra, and numerous buffet tables and bars scattered around the room. At one point, I went up to the buffet to get some dinner. After I had prepared my plate, I headed back to our table and noticed a man standing about ten feet away looking in my direction who looked like he might be the banquet manager. Though it was a little dark, I quickly realized that this man was the principal at my elementary school. I had no idea he did this for a second income and could not have been more surprised. But I quickly went back to my table and wondered how I could face him at school on Monday morning. I was sure he had questions about how I had been invited to this event and ended up at one of the premium tables.

The following Monday, I was able to get to my classroom without running into the principal and quickly found my good friend, LaWanda. I was sure she had already found out about Saturday night and could give me some advice on what to say to our boss. I could tell by the look on her face that she knew everything and probably had already had a long talk with the principal. When I asked her about it, she said he asked her what she knew about me being at the fund-raiser and how I got invited. Even though she knew everything, she told him she didn't have any idea. He would just have to ask me about it himself. I couldn't believe she threw me under the bus like that but I could tell she was really enjoying seeing me in this uncomfortable position. I asked her if he would say anything, and she said she didn't think he would because it really wasn't any of his business, and I hadn't done anything wrong, so what was there to say? Though he never said anything to me about that night, I felt he never looked at me the same again.

As the rest of the school year went on, we continued going to numerous functions and parties within these two social groups. Balancing our social life with my work schedule was exhausting, but I was enjoying it all and somehow able to make it work. When summer arrived, it all came to a close, and it was nice to slow down the pace and take a few trips and attend the occasional pool party or dinner party.

Chapter 3

MOVING TO AUSTIN

Every once in a while, we would take a weekend trip to Austin, where James had financial interests in a bank and owned a condo. Unfortunately, the mid-eighties brought with it a recession, with lower oil prices and problems at the bank that I did not fully understand. On one of our return trips to Houston, James informed me that he felt the need to move to Austin to try and keep the bank solvent. He asked me if I would move to Austin as well, but because it was autumn and I was in the middle of my teaching contract, I could not move until the following summer. I was concerned that my car wouldn't be up to making numerous round trips to Austin, but James assured me I could fly back and forth until I could make a permanent move. This went on for a few months until James decided I just needed to get a better car rather than flying back and forth. I went car shopping one weekend and picked out a nice sedan that would safely get me to and from Austin.

After spending a few months in Austin, James decided to buy a house. He found a beautiful four-bedroom home with a pool and magnificent lake, and downtown views. We named it Twin Valley after the street it was on. He asked his Houston housekeeper, Virginia, if she would be interested in moving to Austin to continue working for him. She leaped at the opportunity. Virginia helped him with the move and quickly got him settled in his new surroundings. We kept our season tickets to the ballet, opera, and symphony in Houston, so James would frequently come to Houston on the weekend. This enabled us to split the travel responsibility evenly, taking a lot of the burden off of me.

I applied for a teaching job in Austin and, by spring, had secured a position with an east-side school. While we were talking about my moving plans, James mentioned that we would find a nice apartment for me. But since we had now been together for over four years, I thought maybe it was time for me to move in with him. So I said that I already had a nice apartment in Houston and didn't need one in Austin. What about me moving into the house? This was a big commitment for James, and he needed to give it some serious consideration. After a few weeks, he decided it made sense, and he was willing to give it a try. After a summer together under the same roof, James appeared very happy with the arrangement, and we continued living together from then on.

Another significant change for James was his decision to get a dog. I don't know what prompted him to do this, as he had never mentioned it before. He asked me what kind of dog I liked, and I said I'd grown up with golden retrievers. He had grown up with a German shepherd. I didn't know which way he was leaning. He began searching newspaper ads and soon found a two-year-old golden whose owners had moved to Austin to go to the university and were now living in a small apartment unsuitable for their large dog. Tristan came for a visit, and we decided he would be a wonderful addition to our home. He began his life with us as an outside dog, but after a few weeks had easily worked his way into the house and quickly adapted to his new life. My moving into the house, and the addition of a dog, were both significant changes for James, but he seemed very happy and content, and we were living a wonderful life.

Since James was an only child, introducing him to my family, which included seven siblings, would need to be done slowly and carefully. His first introduction to my family was when my mother and one of my sisters visited us for a long weekend. Originally, my mother and

I had scheduled a trip to NYC for her birthday so she could see some shows, but she didn't feel she had the energy for such a large city, and I thought a trip to Austin would be easier for her. They really enjoyed coming to Austin as neither one had been to Texas before. A friend of ours was a tour guide in Austin and said he would bring the bus by our house to pick up my mother and sister before beginning his next tour so they could see the local sights and learn about Austin's history. I joined them because I was sure there were things I didn't know about my city. I enjoyed the tour more than I thought I would because our friend was so entertaining and a wonderful storyteller. After dropping off everyone else at the end of the tour, he brought us back to the house. We thanked him for providing us with this unexpected treat. What a great way of getting introduced to Austin.

We tried our best to come up with other experiences my sister and mother would enjoy that would create some wonderful memories from their visit. Since my mother's side of the family was German, we took her to Fredericksburg, a town well known for its German heritage. My mother really enjoyed walking around town and visiting the many shops on the main street. We stopped by one of the restaurants famous for its German cuisine, which really pleased my mother. On the way back to Austin, we passed by the LBJ Ranch, where they could see longhorn cattle up close.

James was such a wonderful host and, on Saturday morning, made something I had not heard about before. As the father of three, James was well known at home for making special pancakes in the shape of animals. My mother and sister found this delightful, and I was amazed because I had never seen him do this before and was honored that he would do it for my family. My mother returned the favor when she asked James what his favorite pie was. He said lemon meringue, and she made one from scratch. He loved it. We had planned to host a party for the opera at our house that evening, so my family was able to meet a lot of our friends and could tell this was one of the reasons why we loved living in Austin. I was so happy that we made this trip for my mother; it was less than a month later that she suffered a stroke, and though she survived, she was never able to travel again. This trip provided a lot of wonderful memories of spending time together in Austin.

Now it was time to visit the rest of the family, and we planned a trip to Minnesota to celebrate my sister's engagement. James thought it would be nice to do a car trip, even though I told him there was nothing to see between Austin and Minneapolis. James said he loved car trips and had never driven this route before, so we began making plans. He said he knew someone in Kansas City, so we could stop there the first night and complete the trip the next day.

When we arrived in Minneapolis, James said he wanted to take my mother out to lunch and asked me to find out where she would like to go. When I asked her, and she told me, I asked if we could please go somewhere else, but she was insistent. So I let James know that we were going to the American Legion for lunch and to prepare himself for a true Minnesota experience. The Legion serves Minnesota comfort food and is in an older building that has not seen much updating over the years but is very popular with the locals. We picked my mother up and arrived at the Legion for what I thought was going to be a luncheon for just the three of us. But when we went in, we were brought to a table for seven. Without saying anything to us, my mother had invited two of her sisters and their husbands, and I then realized we had been set up. As much as I loved seeing my aunts and uncles, I wished I had been able to prepare James ahead of time for this surprise get-together. I knew what was going on and was confident my mother had at some point told her sisters about our lunch plans and that they had insisted on joining us so they could meet James. The luncheon went very well; James actually loves comfort food, so he didn't have any problem finding something on the menu that he liked. We left the restaurant and brought my mother home, so I was finally able to get James' reaction to the lunch and unexpectedly meeting some of my relatives. He said he enjoyed it, that everyone seemed to have a good time, and he felt well treated. I asked him what he was talking about with my uncles, and he said he learned from Prairie Home Companion that when you don't know what to say, you talk about pickup trucks and the weather, and those were two topics James knew a lot about.

The next evening, we invited my mom and all of my brothers and sisters and their spouses to our hotel room for drinks before going down the street to an engagement party for my sister at the top of one of Minneapolis' high-rise buildings. We arranged with the hotel to have some beer and wine placed on ice in the guest bathroom sink, and as my siblings arrived, James was introduced to the rest of the family. We soon left for dinner, and since our group was quite large, we secured a private dining room with stunning views of downtown and the sunset. The only problem was that the AC was out in this dining room, and they placed a large fan near the door to blow cooler air in from the main restaurant. But once it was sunset, it actually was quite comfortable, and we were able to enjoy the dinner. James and I were hosting this event, so we sat at each end of the table. We had arranged to have numerous flower bouquets placed down the center of the table. Everyone seemed to be having a wonderful time; it was a treat for many of them, who rarely came downtown for dinner. And no one had ever been to this restaurant before to enjoy the spectacular views. James especially seemed to enjoy having dinner with such a large family and was pleased to see how well everyone got along, which made it a very pleasant experience for him. Before everyone left, I let the ladies know that we had a bouquet for each of them to take home to enjoy, and they were quite surprised and pleased by the thoughtful gesture. We left the next day to begin our car trip back to Texas and spent much of the time talking about members of my family. James had enjoyed meeting them.

Since James had such a good time with my family during this visit, it wasn't difficult for him to agree to go back to Minnesota a few years later for my brother's wedding. This time James was going to meet more of my extended family, which included numerous aunts, uncles, and cousins. My brother and his fiancée decided to invite family only to the wedding service; friends and relatives would be invited to the reception following the ceremony. I was a little surprised when my brother called to ask me if I would read a passage from the Bible during the wedding ceremony and if James would consider reading the second passage. At first, I didn't know what to say because James was not big on going to church, much less a Catholic one. I wasn't sure he would be comfortable going up to read from the Bible. When I asked him about it, he said he was honored to be considered family and would be happy to do it.

The wedding was going to be in February, and we thought we'd better bring our fur coats, as the weather can be brutal that time of year. The first night, we went to the rehearsal dinner and had the fur coats in the car with us. But when we arrived at the venue and looked at some of the people going in, we had second thoughts about wearing them. My brother had selected a sports bar for this dinner, and everyone was dressed very casually. We thought the fur coats would be pushing it and decided to leave them in the car. The place was packed; this was James' first experience in a sports bar, and he was surprised to see so many TVs all around the bar. Fortunately, we had a semi-private room reserved for our dinner where it wasn't so loud, and we could easily hear everyone. Still, there were a lot of TVs in the room. They all were showing the Winter Olympic events, which were going on at the time.

By now, James had spent enough time with my family that he felt comfortable in the group and had no difficulty holding his own. It helped that my family didn't have much knowledge about James' background; they considered him a part of our family, so they treated him that way, and he quickly became one of us. We remained at the dinner for many hours, during which time my brother and his fiancée opened some of the gifts. I didn't tell my brother ahead of time, but I remembered him asking one day about our grandfather's shillelagh that he'd gotten in Ireland and had hanging in his kitchen. My brother wondered what happened to it after our grandfather passed away. I said I didn't know as I was in Houston at the time and had no idea what had happened to his belongings. So when he opened our gift, he looked at me with this surprised look and said this couldn't be what he thought it was. I let him know

I was the one who asked for the shillelagh and had had it all this time and decided it was time to pass it on to him. My brother told the group about the story behind this gift so they could understand why he was so emotional about it and how much it meant to him to receive it after so many years of not knowing what had happened to it. After a while, we decided to leave and said our good-byes as our downtown hotel was almost an hour away.

Though the wedding was going to be in a small town out in the country, my brother and his fiancée wanted it to be formal, so we were required to wear tuxedos. We arrived at the church, which was small but very charming, and the inside was beautifully decorated with flowers in various shades of red with white and green accents. There were only a couple dozen people in attendance, and it was a lovely ceremony that moved along very quickly. For some reason, the reception, which was nearby, didn't start for another hour, so we asked what we were going to do. Because we were in such a small town, the only option was to return to the sports bar from the night before. In the car, James asked if they were serious about going back to the bar, and I said yes because there really isn't anything else to do in this small town. He asked how we could go in there when we were all dressed so formally, and everyone else would be casually dressed. I just said, "Well, welcome to my family and to life in small-town Minnesota." We arrived at the bar and watched as my brother helped his bride get out of the white limousine in her long dress with the veil and train thrown over her arm, and we followed them inside. To James' surprise, no one even looked up at us, as if this was a common occurrence on Saturday afternoons. Then James was even more surprised to see the bride drinking a long neck while in her wedding dress. He now wondered if this was what it was like in Lake Wobegon because he could imagine Garrison Keillor walking in and describing this scene for one of the radio programs James so much enjoyed.

After about an hour, we left to go on to the reception, which was being held nowhere else but at the local American Legion. When we arrived, it looked like most of the people had already arrived because it was busy with loud music playing in the background. We went over to the wedding-party table, where James and I had assigned seats, and enjoyed a great view of the room. I pointed out who some of my family members were, and because we had such a large family, they easily made up about half the group. The two aunts and uncles from the luncheon a few years ago were there, so James recognized a few familiar faces.

We didn't have to wait very long before dinner was served, and everyone got settled at their tables. After a few speeches and some toasts to the couple, we finished our dinner, and they began preparing the room for dancing. James decided that he felt most comfortable staying where he was as he had a good vantage point for watching everyone. But one of my mother's sisters came up to James and said that since he was family, he needed to come down to her table to join everyone else. I really appreciated this because it made James feel really special, and it also gave me time to go around and say hello to many of my cousins and other family members that I didn't get to see very often and not leave James alone. James seemed to really enjoy becoming a member of a new family much larger than what he'd grown up with, and we would enjoy many more times of getting together with the family in Minnesota.

Shortly after we returned from this trip, the bank failed. Texas was going through a recession. James was left with the responsibility of paying off significant debts because his partner was sent to prison. In the process, he sold off some of his assets, including the condos in NYC, Ft. Lauderdale, and Aspen. His favorite was the Aspen condo, so it was the last one to go. We went on our last New Year's trip to Aspen to attend the usual parties, including the New Year's Day brunch he co-hosted with Dorothy, a condo neighbor. They had a friendly competition as to who could invite the biggest celebrity. James invited a friend of ours, former playmate Barbi Benton and her husband, and Dorothy invited Brooke Shields' mother, Teri. Because Teri didn't bring Brooke along with her (she was in Aspen but went skiing instead), James was the confirmed winner. It was one of our best Aspen trips—and our last one at the condo, which sold the following spring.

Austin grew quite rapidly as the recession let up. The introduction of many tech companies helped make Austin's economy much stronger. With this growth came an improved arts scene, with a new conductor for the symphony, new artistic directors for the ballet and regional theatre, a growing opera company, and a new performing arts hall. The quality of the performances had improved so much that we didn't feel the need to travel to Houston for the arts and began devoting our interests locally. James quickly became a well-known philanthropist, and we were invited to numerous events around town. We were meeting a lot of new people involved in various arts organizations and were simply referred to as James and Larry by our growing circle of friends, something that didn't happen in Houston. James thought I should begin getting involved with some of these groups by joining some of the boards and taking on some leadership positions, including chairing some fund-raisers, which was a new experience for me. With the growth of these organizations came ample opportunities to contribute to a number of fund-raisers and capital campaigns. James was able to make significant gifts that came with impressive naming opportunities. The first one was with the opera company, which was raising money to open a new building with a music school. James made the first large gift and was invited to attach his name to the building or the school. He chose the music school, which turned out to be fortuitous because the opera ended up selling the building after a number of years, and the music school ventured out on its own. To this day is still called the Armstrong Community Music School.

The second opportunity came with the ballet, which was renovating a building to create a new home downtown. With James' gift, one of the studios was named after us, which became the first time our names would be displayed together in a public building. Other naming opportunities included the main staircase at the performing arts hall, a dedicated exhibit at the new children's museum, a bedroom at the local hospice organization, and a lounge in the new bed tower at the children's hospital. James' last two major gifts were for an education endowment for the children's programs at the symphony and a variety of places within the new theatre where I was a board member. James' philosophy about giving was that it was important to put his name out there to show people his donation was for a worthy cause, and he hoped it would inspire others to contribute. He also wanted to give as much as he could while he was living so he could enjoy the fruits of his philanthropy.

With our involvement in financially helping improve the arts, education, and health services in Austin came the opportunity to be recognized and appreciated with various awards. One of the first was when the opera wanted to honor James at their 25th Anniversary Gala. This began with a proclamation from the city naming February 23, 2008, James C. Armstrong Day. A large number of opera donors attended the ceremony at City Hall, where the mayor read the proclamation making it official. On the night of the gala, the opera arranged for us to be picked up in a beautifully restored classic car. We arrived at the hotel and went down to the reception area. We were taken aback by one of the auction items on display. It was a large painting of James and me with a circle of beautiful women toasting champagne. This image was also used for the cover of the program, which became a treasured keepsake. My only regret of the evening was not bidding on the painting, but it did go to some very good friends. The rest of the evening was fun and entertaining, and I believe that with the other auction items, table sales, and monetary donations, it was one of the opera's most successful fund-raisers.

Some other awards we received included being named to the Austin Arts Hall of Fame for the Critics Table Awards, the Ballet Austin Bravos Award, and the Outstanding Philanthropists award for our local AFP organization (Association of Fundraising Professionals). Our acceptance speech for this last award was as follows:

We would first like to thank Stefania Tafuro and ZACH Theatre for initiating the nomination for this award, along with the support of other organizations that offered their endorsements—we are truly humbled.

Though we have been recognized for some major gifts to the arts and education, what we try to model by example is the importance of annual giving, participation, and support to these organizations. Whether it is a monetary gift, volunteering time on boards, projects, and committees, season tickets, or contributing to galas and fund-raising efforts; there are so many opportunities for everyone to give.

Now I'm not above promoting one event while at another, and I can't tell you the constraint I'm using, not to mention Zach Scott's Red, Hot & Soul on February 27th … but I won't. But it is this idea of crossover where we are beginning to witness a stronger sense of collaboration among organizations where they share ideas, resources, and talent that benefit everyone involved. We hope to see this trend continue.

Our goal in all of this is to do what we can to help make Austin the kind of place we want to live in. Thank you to the AFP for this wonderful honor and to our friends who joined us today. We are truly appreciative to you for this award.

Thank you.

A particular highlight for us was receiving the Humanitarian Award from our local Anti-Defamation League at their Torch of Liberty gala. Here is the ADL introduction:

First, I would like to thank my parents for allowing me to participate in this presentation on behalf of our family, and I would like to tell my parents what an incredible legacy they are leaving for their children and grandchildren.

This year's recipients of the Audrey and Raymond Maislin Humanitarian Award are James Armstrong and Larry

Connelly. Since it is impossible in this short period of time to summarize all of James' and Larry's contributions, I will focus instead on how James and Larry have furthered greater harmony and cooperation in our communities, which is why this award is being given to them.

When my parents asked me to present this award, I called my great friend and mentor, Cookie Ruiz, the Executive Director of Ballet Austin, and a prior recipient of this award, to get additional insights on James and Larry. According to Cookie, James and Larry are so very special because they are transformational givers who allow an organization to accomplish and realize a full vision for its future. Cookie also noted that James and Larry allow their names to go on projects, which gives the recipient organization credibility and makes the job of raising additional funds infinitely easier.

As I look around the Austin community, I see the Armstrong School of Music at the Austin Lyric Opera, the endowment to the Austin Symphony to support its youth programs, and the Armstrong/Connelly Studio at Ballet Austin's Butler Community School. There is an Armstrong Family Auditorium on the drawing board for Zachary Scott Theatre.

At a recent community open house that Ballet Austin hosted, I witnessed hundreds of people of all ages and from all parts of the Austin community doing the hula in the Armstrong/Connelly studio. It was a vision of harmony and cooperation.

James and Larry, you have given your time, your money, and your hearts to our community. It is my great honor and privilege to present this award to you.

After this beautiful introduction, it was my turn to say something for James and me. This is what I said:

> We want to thank the Torch of Liberty Committee for this prestigious honor. We were quite surprised when we received word of this and are humbled to have our names associated with such great people as the Maislins and the ADL organization.
>
> Our philanthropic goals in providing resources and time to the various arts and education organizations, along with the number of community service organizations we support, is to do what we can to create the kind of city we call home.
>
> Especially an organization that has accepted and recognized us over the past nearly twenty-six years for what we have accomplished as a couple …
>
> [At this point I was taken aback when the audience broke out into a round of applause, a reaction I was not expecting; I was very touched and barely able to finish.]
>
> a core value of the ADL which we so appreciate, do not take for granted, and for which we are most grateful.
>
> Thank you so much for this recognition and to our friends who have supported us tonight and in turn, the extraordinary causes of the ADL.

This award was presented in a packed ballroom filled with a large and prestigious group of Austinites, letting us know how appreciative they were of us and how accepting they were of our relationship. It was one of the most touching experiences we'd had since moving to Austin.

There was one deficiency in Austin we couldn't fix through our philanthropy, and it was related to one of James' favorite pastimes. For many years, beginning with his time in Midland, James enjoyed collecting cars, with a special interest in Rolls Royce. When he left Midland, he brought his collection with him to Houston, where he had to store most of them but always kept at least one at his house. There was an automotive maintenance company that specialized in luxury cars, so James had his favorite mechanic, Garfield, available to take care of the numerous repairs these cars were famous for, usually related to battery issues. All of this worked well until we moved to Austin, which, due to its small size at the time, had no place to store or take care of his collection. But because of the bank failure, he decided it was time to sell off his fleet, keeping just one Rolls Royce in Austin. When the car had any issues, James would have to have it trucked to Houston to get repaired, then truck it back to Austin. This went on for a few years until one day when James was driving down Lamar and passing the intersection at Twenty-Fourth Street, the car stopped. He tried everything he could think of but could not get it started again. While going through this ordeal, he didn't realize that a police car had rolled up behind him. The officer offered assistance, but the car would not start and needed to be towed. Due to the size of this car, it required a special-sized trailer that would take some time before it arrived. Since it was quite warm outside, the officer offered for James to get into the patrol car to wait, but he was reluctant to do so. What if someone he knew drove by and saw him in the back seat of the patrol car and wondered what he had done to get pulled over in his Rolls Royce? He was so upset by this whole experience that by the time he got the car towed and was back home, he'd decided to call his mechanic in Houston to come and get the car and said he wanted to sell it. That would be the last time he owned a Rolls Royce but still remained a lifetime member of the Rolls Royce Club. He read each of their publications that came in the mail on a quarterly basis and, from time to time, would attend car meets around the country.

It wasn't until many years later, after Austin saw a huge growth in the population that someone opened a luxury car dealership that included Bentleys and Rolls Royces. James first saw some of these cars at an auto show he attended each year. This was all he needed to get "the bug." He decided he wanted to get another luxury car, this time a Bentley. We made an appointment to go out to the dealership and were shown many models. In the end, James decided on a convertible in gray with a red interior, but he wanted to take a test drive first. I didn't think they would let anyone take these cars out onto the streets. Surely it would be one of the employees doing the driving. But they said that we could take it out and someone would ride with us to answer any questions. I did not like this response; since James didn't drive anymore, it meant I would be the one behind the wheel. I was really nervous about driving a car this expensive and really didn't want to do this. But James was insistent, and the salesman said we could stay on the side streets until I was more comfortable. So we got in for my first Bentley experience. It took a while for me to get used to the car because it was really powerful, but at the same time, the smoothest ride I had ever experienced in a car. Eventually, I was comfortable enough to take it out on the freeway, and it was an amazing experience. I was happy when we returned to the dealership because now that the pressure was off, I felt like I was taking my first breath since we'd left. James decided he wanted the car, and they said they would get it cleaned up and we could pick it up in a couple of days. This provided us with time to get the money together and for them to get all the paperwork prepared for taking the trade-in, and for James to take ownership of his new Bentley.

We brought the car home and really enjoyed taking it out for rides, but after a few days, James said he didn't know if he was comfortable having such an expensive car sitting in the garage. He asked if I would call the dealership to see if we could return it. I could only imagine how the salesman was going to take the news because not only was James returning this car, we would want our trade-in back in its place. When I called our salesman, I could tell he was upset. But he was very professional. He said he wanted to make sure James was certain about his decision because they already had the trade-in cleaned up and had prepared a page to sell it on their website. I said James was sure, and he asked me to bring the car back the next day. Of course, James wouldn't go back with me, and I had to face the salesman by myself. I was sure we would not be back to see any cars at this dealership for a very long while, but that would not be the case.

It wasn't two days later when James said he'd changed his mind again. He really wanted the Bentley back. He really liked it and couldn't stop thinking about it. He asked me if I would call the salesman again. I said I would under one condition: he had to promise me he wouldn't change his mind again for at least two years because I was not going to go through this again until at least that much time had passed. He promised, so I made the call. This time, the salesman was really not happy. I assured him that James was serious about this and said he'd promised me he would keep the car for at least two years. The salesman said that this had happened before, so he had known to keep all the paperwork for a few days and still had everything in his possession. He agreed to let me come in the next day with the trade-in, and we would make the switch. Fortunately, James kept his promise, and we were invited to numerous events at the dealership. We became friends with the salesman, who turned out to be the manager, and even traded in this Bentley for a new sedan before James stopped purchasing any more luxury cars.

But there is one more car story that was true to James' nature. We usually had a third car we would refer to as the "dog's car." This would normally be an SUV that would be used to transfer our dog or when we needed the extra room to transport things we purchased in larger amounts. One year we had a Chevrolet and went out to run errands. We were only a couple of blocks away from our house before we had to stop to wait for a garbage truck to move because it was blocking the street. We were at least fifty yards behind the truck. Unexpectedly, the driver began backing up. I was certain he would stop because there really wasn't anything where we were parked. But he kept backing up, and before I knew it, he was backing over the hood of our car and began pushing it back. Somehow the other person in the truck saw what was happening and got the driver to stop. We weren't hurt, but the front of our car up to the windshield was completely destroyed. The driver came around and profusely apologized and said he would call his supervisor. It wasn't long before there were at least five city vehicles surrounding us on the scene. The supervisor said the city would cover all costs, and he gave us his contact information. He asked us to call our dealership to make the arrangements to pick up the car and make the necessary repairs. As we were working out the details, I noticed James starting to walk away toward our home, and I called for him to wait. I went over to him and asked what he was doing. He said he didn't want this car anymore and had decided to go home. I said we couldn't just leave it there; we needed to deal with it. He said I could work out the details, and he would be home when I was finished. James just didn't like to deal with any type of conflict and was happy to leave it up to me to work things out. What a guy!

Another of James' hobbies was real estate, where he searched for homes to add to his collection of rental properties or sometimes just toured larger homes on the market with a real estate friend. One day James mentioned he thought he'd found another house to purchase. I assumed he was talking about another rental property until he said he thought we could move in by June. I was completely caught off guard because James had stated many times that we were not moving from Twin Valley, and he had never mentioned he was interested in finding a new home. He said what he really liked about this new house was that it had a lot of wall space to display his art collection, something we couldn't do in this house, where many pieces of his collection were in closets and under beds. The new house was twice as big, though it only had three bedrooms and an apartment next to the garage. He said we could look at it this weekend to see if I liked it. We made the appointment, and I was amazed when I saw the architecture, lake and hill country views, and the beautiful pool. In total, the house was on five levels but had an elevator for three of the main floors. James said that since the house had been on the market for four years, he was in no hurry. He would think about it over the weekend and let the realtor know of his decision by Monday. We talked about the house all weekend and, in the end, decided to go ahead with the purchase.

When James called his realtor with the news, he was surprised to find out that someone had seen the house the day before and made an offer on it. We were really disappointed but felt it was just not meant to be. A week later, James' realtor called with surprising news. The potential buyer had backed out of the deal, and the house was back on the market. James, knowing that the house had been on the market for four years, made a significantly lower offer. The bank, excited to finally have a serious buyer, eagerly accepted his offer and even provided him with a sizable allowance to make some changes and updates.

It took the movers about four days to pack up Twin Valley. On moving day, I headed to the new house (El Greco) with the movers behind me, and James waited until they had everything loaded and he could secure Twin Valley. At El Greco, I could see the moving trucks just a few blocks away. As they came up the hill, the skies opened up with a torrential downpour. I waited on the covered porch as the movers came up to the house to ask me what we were going to do. I saw James drive up and said we would wait for him to find out what the plan would be. But to my surprise, James stayed in his car because he didn't want to confront the movers to determine what we were going to do. I couldn't believe he was going to let me handle this alone. I pulled up my big-boy pants and let the drivers know we were going to move in today one way or another because we didn't have any place to sleep that night. It was already late in the day, so we didn't have a large window of time to accomplish this task. Luckily the rain stopped within the hour, and we prepared the front hall by covering the floors to protect them from getting too wet and began the move-in process. James eventually got out of his car and joined us, grinning and not at all ashamed of putting me in a difficult situation.

It took a few weeks before we were completely settled in. James brought in a friend from NYC who worked in the art world to help him decide where the artwork would best be displayed. It was well worth it to bring her in because this turned out to be a daunting task that would have been difficult for us to accomplish. She did such a great job that in the twenty-five years we spent in this house, we never moved any of the art.

This home made it a lot easier to host parties, which we frequently did. One of the first ones came about after James sold the Aspen condo. A few days after the following Christmas, James announced that he wanted to have a New Year's Day brunch like we'd done in Aspen. He wanted a similar menu of ham, chili, grits, black-eyed peas, and cornbread, with Bloody Marys and champagne. I expressed my concern that it was only a few days away, that I had never made chili or black-eyed peas, and that I wasn't even sure what grits were or how they were prepared. He said Virginia could help and proceeded to create a guest list that totaled about fifty names. I really didn't know how this was going to work out, but I started looking for recipes while he began calling our guests. I was surprised that on such short notice, about forty people said they would love to attend. When they asked what they could bring, James suggested that they bring a dessert. I found the recipes I needed, completed the shopping for ingredients, and blindly began the cooking process. We worked together to locate enough dishes, silverware, napkins, and glassware for forty, mixing and matching along the way. Surprisingly, on the day of the party, things went smoothly, and our guests had a wonderful time. We did overdo it in the dessert department. We ended up with over two-dozen different desserts, creating a lot of leftovers. We made notes along the way and decided we would do it again the next year—and wouldn't ask all the guests to bring a dessert.

We continued this New Year's tradition for many years, adding to the guest list as our group of friends grew each year. As the popularity of this brunch expanded, I told James it was becoming too much for Virginia and me to pull off successfully. As we approached sixty guests, we decided it was time to bring in a catering company. They were able to create the same menu with some additions and brought in needed staff, including bartenders, as well as rented dishes and glassware. This was a much better process. I could now enjoy the party, and Virginia could supervise the kitchen. We continued this tradition for a few more years, limiting the guest list to seventy-five friends.

One year James found a Christmas/New Year's cruise to the Caribbean that looked like a lot of fun. We made the reservations and left out of Miami, stopping at numerous islands, including what would be my favorite, Barbados. The ship was beautiful, and we had a lot of fun with the planned activities. We also met some great people with whom we enjoyed spending time. We arrived back in Austin a few weeks later for me to return to teaching and discovered that a number of our friends had been talking about us. Apparently, word got around town that some people did not receive their invitation to our New Year's brunch and wondered what they had done to be removed from the guest list. We never thought about people expecting this brunch to be an annual event that they were looking forward to it every year. James had to spend the next few days calling people to let them know they were not excluded and telling them about our trip over the holidays. He assured them we would have the brunch next year, and they would make the guest list.

After a few more years of hosting this party, we decided to switch to a holiday party in mid-December instead of the New Year's brunch. Our living room had a vaulted ceiling, so we were able to fit a twelve-foot tree, which was the centerpiece of the party and took over two days to decorate with a minimum of 1,800 lights. We would spend days decorating the house, adding a lot of outdoor lighting to create a memorable festive atmosphere. We were the first people on our street to decorate this much in our neighborhood, and after a few years, most of the neighborhood was beautifully lighted. This party was as successful as the brunch, and the guest list grew each year. The highlight for us was when our friend Anton Nel, an internationally renowned classical pianist, would play our piano for a short concert each year.

We frequently hosted dinner parties, which was our favorite way to entertain friends. The flow of the main level and the size of the living room allowed us to host many fund-raisers and larger dinner parties. One of our goals for these parties was to mix up the guest lists to include people from various groups in our social circles to make the parties more interesting. We usually had some form of entertainment; musicians enjoyed playing in that space because the vaulted ceiling provided wonderful acoustics for their music. During the summer, we also invited friends to come to the pool on Sundays. It was a nice way to have friends over because everything we needed was down at the pool level. We had a room with AC and a bathroom for changing, so we never had to go into the house. All in all, El Greco proved itself many times over as a great party house, perfect for many forms of entertainment.

Chapter 4

EXTRAORDINARY TRIPS

We traveled a lot during our thirty-three years together, but there were a few trips that stand out. Trying to describe these experiences will be difficult, but I will attempt to do them justice.

Buckingham Palace I & II

We frequently traveled with an agent in NYC (Susan) who was well connected throughout the world and able to put together truly once-in-a-lifetime experiences. One day in the fall of 2000, she called and said she had a special invitation for twenty people for a week in London and asked if we would we be interested in joining her. The trip centered on a reception, concert, and seated dinner at Buckingham Palace with Prince Charles, who was hosting a benefit for one of his charities, the Monteverdi Choir. Though we were not familiar with this group, we couldn't pass up the opportunity to attend. Over the next few months, Susan completed the guest list and created a week's worth of tours and activities to make this trip even more memorable.

But the evening with Prince Charles was definitely the high point. Our group approached the palace in a line of cars and, after going through all of the security measures we arrived at the main entrance.

Since we didn't know exactly how this was going to play out, we stayed close together. We climbed the main staircase up to a beautiful reception area for cocktails. There were a number of rooms where we were allowed to roam, but we were told to stay close to Susan because she had something special planned specifically for our group. After about an hour, our group was invited to a private room and asked to form a reception line because we were about to individually be introduced to Prince Charles. After a few minutes, a door opened at the end of the room, and, as promised, Prince Charles walked in with an entourage, and he approached our group. He walked up to each of us to welcome us to the palace, to thank us for supporting his charity, and to have a picture taken with each of us as he shook our hands. I never dreamed of this happening and was quite nervous as he slowly moved down the line and approached me. When James and I said we were from Austin, he talked briefly about his visit to Austin a number of years earlier. To this day, I can vividly remember this amazing moment and currently have the photo displayed in my home. As he continued down the line, I looked around and noticed the entourage that followed him into the room but kept their distance. One of the members stood out because it was Camilla, who was currently dating the prince but had not yet married him. Throughout the evening, she traveled in his group but seemed to keep her distance, placing the focus of the evening on him.

After the reception, we were ushered into the concert hall, which was an addition to the original palace. It is a beautiful room with high ceilings, and a massive pipe organ on one end that we were told did not currently work, but there were plans to refurbish it in the near future. On the other end of the room was a stage for the Monteverdi Choir. This group of musicians only played instruments from the period of Monteverdi's life and had prepared a concert with four soloists. The acoustics were phenomenal, and the music was beautiful and moving.

After the concert, we were directed into the room next door for a seated dinner. It turned out to be the Queen's Portrait Gallery, which was ornately decorated with numerous portraits on every wall. Multiple tables for ten were scattered around the room, with a larger head table for the prince and his guests in the center of the room. Once we located our table, we waited for the other guests to arrive and noticed an empty seat between James and myself. We didn't recognize the name and wondered who it might be. Once she arrived, we immediately recognized her as the lead soloist for the Monteverdi Choir and a Brooke Shields look-alike. She was very friendly and gracious, and we were honored to have her join our table. The other table guests were equally gracious. We enjoyed looking around the room and admiring the beautiful flowers, uniformed palace staff (five per table), and sumptuous decor. As per protocol, no one began eating until the prince had begun.

After dinner, Prince Charles stood up to make a few remarks and to introduce us to a surprise treat. Recently, an unknown piece of music composed by Monteverdi had been discovered. A Monteverdi Choir violinist played this music for us on a violin once owned by Monteverdi. It was a moving piece of music played beautifully. This was a perfect ending to an amazing evening. We returned to our hotel, still trying to process everything we had experienced that evening. The rest of the week was filled with numerous private tours of some of London's better-known attractions, along with lunches and dinners at private clubs and various locations normally closed to the public. It was the holiday season, so all of these venues, including our hotel, were beautifully decorated, making this trip even more memorable for us.

We thought of this trip as a once-in-a-lifetime experience, but in the spring of 2005, we were surprised to get another invitation to Buckingham Palace. This time, Susan received an invitation to another fundraiser for one of Prince Charles' philanthropic groups, a dinner, and a concert with the Philharmonia Orchestra. This trip was going to be during the first week of May, and since I was just completing my first year as an elementary principal in a local school district, I needed to get permission from my assistant superintendent to take the week off. I called her and said I had a tremendous favor to ask. I told her that I'd been offered an amazing opportunity. Could I take the first week off in May to go to London and have dinner with Prince Charles at Buckingham Palace? There was dead silence on the other end of the phone. I said, "Beverly, are you still there?" She finally responded, saying she needed a moment to process what I had just asked of her. She replied that due to some recent personal changes in her life, she had developed the philosophy that one should always take unique opportunities when they present themselves. Then she said, if it had been anyone else who asked her for this request, she wouldn't have believed it. But because it was me who was asking, she knew it was real and granted me the time off. I was so relieved because I had no idea how she was going to respond.

This time, we were better prepared for what we were about to experience. Now, however, Prince Charles was married to Camilla, so she would be more present and accessible. When we arrived at the palace, we went up to the same reception area, but there didn't seem to be as many people. Then I noticed some people were going off to an area that seemed more remote, and I followed them. It turned out that there was a larger reception area, and Prince Charles was mingling with everyone in this room. So I went to get James, and we joined the larger group, which was in a beautiful room that overlooked the private gardens. As we were looking through the windows, Susan joined us and asked if we had gone up to meet Camilla yet. We said we hadn't and weren't sure we would. She insisted and told us that all we needed to do was to give our names to the lady-in-waiting, and we would be introduced. We walked up toward where Camilla was standing, but as we got closer, the assistant walked away, leaving Camilla standing by herself. We weren't sure what to do, so we just walked up, said hello, gave our names, and told her where we were from. She thanked us for traveling so far to support her husband's charity. I said, "Oh no, we traveled this far to see you, and by the way, you look amazing this evening." She kind of blushed but graciously thanked us as we moved away.

We were directed to the concert hall, where the orchestra was on stage. The conductor announced that they had a special treat for us. The pipe organ had just recently been restored, and tonight they would play it for the first time for one of their music selections. It was truly magical to be there at that moment, appreciating how they had provided such a unique experience for our group—one that few people would ever have. We did not take this experience for granted and thoroughly enjoyed the rest of the concert.

Dinner was served in another part of the palace that consisted of a series of smaller rooms connected to each other, so we couldn't see everything that was going on, but the decor, service, and food were as amazing as we had expected. We returned to our hotel feeling very special and reminisced about all we had experienced that evening. We'd invited two people from our group to join us for dinner the next evening at our hotel, so we went to the restaurant to make the reservation. When you are at the Ritz, they constantly say that as a guest, you can have anything you want, so we felt pretty confident about our dinner plans. We arrived at the maitre d' station and asked for a table for four at eight the next evening. After looking at the reservation book, the maitre d' told us that would be impossible and that he had no tables available. When we said we were guests of the hotel, he again replied that he was sorry but still had no tables. We were quite surprised by his response but not ready to give up. We went back to the lobby to the concierge desk to see if they could help. We've always said these guys were the best and have never disappointed us. We told the man at the desk what had just happened, and he said, "But you are guests of the hotel, so of course, you can have a table." I told him that the maitre d' didn't seem to understand this policy, and was there anything he could do? A gentleman was standing nearby listening to all of this and asked if there was anything wrong. I told him that we didn't have any trouble getting a table for dinner at Buckingham Palace this evening, but we couldn't get one here for tomorrow night. He asked if we were guests of the hotel, and I said yes. He told the concierge that he would see what he could do, and we returned with him to the restaurant. We didn't know who this gentleman was, but he was very friendly and asked about our stay at the hotel.

As we continued talking and walking through the lobby to the restaurant, which is almost a block long, he took out a business card and said to feel free to contact him if we had any other problems during our stay at the hotel. I looked down at the card and was surprised to see that he was the director of the hotel and thought about how we were witnessing something amazing. When we got to the restaurant, the maitre d' looked up and saw James and me and almost rolled his eyes until he looked over at who was standing next to us. His face quickly went pale as he slowly rose. Our new friend said he understood that we had requested a table for the next evening and, as guests of the hotel, were having trouble accomplishing this request. Was there anything he could do? The maitre d' stumbled with the reservation book and turned pages back and forth before confirming that he did indeed have an available table for us. He confirmed the time, our names, and room number and said he would look forward to seeing us. As we walked back, we profusely thanked the gentleman, and, needless to say, we had no problems during the rest of our stay. The next evening we arrived at the restaurant, where the same maitre d' was working and he showed us to our table, which was in the best location near the dance floor and band, facing the entrance. Our friends were impressed, but we didn't tell them about our experience the night before.

The rest of our time in London was spent enjoying various luncheons, dinners, tours, and cocktail receptions created especially for our group. One standout experience was lunch at Kensington Palace, hosted by Prince and Princess Michael of Kent. Another day was spent traveling to Blenheim Palace, hosted by the Duke and Duchess of Marlborough, where we had a private tour of the palace and gardens followed by a lovely seated luncheon. What helped us gain access to many of these private experiences was our connection to the American Museum in Britain, which was also the connection for creating a diverse travel group of people, who were from all over the world, many of whom we would travel with in the future.

Russia

Another amazing travel opportunity came in the fall of 1998 when we received a phone call from a friend in San Francisco. She was coordinating a trip for Gordon Getty to benefit the Russian National Orchestra (RNO), an organization he supported. For a significant contribution, we would fly to NYC, where we would join a group and board Gordon's private plane. We would fly to St. Petersburg and travel by riverboat with the RNO on their three-concert tour in the Volga River region. We would complete the trip with a concert in Moscow. This was a lot of information to process, but in the end, we decided we could not pass up this opportunity to tour Russia in a way that few people have ever dreamed of.

We arrived in NYC a day early to ensure we would not miss getting on Gordon's plane and took this opportunity to finally see The Lion King on Broadway, acquiring excellent seats through our hotel's concierge. We received details on where to board the plane and were impressed when we saw the 727 waiting for us. We boarded and walked around to see how the plane had been retrofitted with large lounges in the front and rear and a master suite in the center. We met the other guests as they arrived and settled in for the trip. There were three attendants on board to provide us with endless drinks and food throughout the evening. Midway on our trip, we stopped at an airport in Ireland to refuel. We had a one-hour break, so we decided to go into the terminal. It was about 2 a.m., and we were surprised to find a pub open with a fair number of people present. As we were waiting to board the plane, I glanced over James' shoulder to see a familiar figure walking toward us. It was Senator Bob Dole. We stopped him as he was walking by and introduced ourselves. After we told him why we were there, we asked him the same question. He said he was on Air Force Two on a special mission for the US government. He didn't provide details, which was understandable, but we did ask if we could take a photo together. He was more than happy to oblige. We noticed that many of our fellow passengers were coming toward us.

We then asked him if we could take a group photo. It surprised me that I was the only one with a camera, and so I was asked by everyone if I would send the group a copy after we returned home. I promised I would.

A short time later, we returned to the plane for the remainder of our trip to St. Petersburg. Once we arrived at the airport, the plane taxied to a secluded spot on the tarmac, where we waited for the authorities to arrive. Our passports were collected and given to someone on the tarmac to check. Once we were cleared, we boarded a waiting bus to take us into town. We noticed two gentlemen boarded the bus with us who were dressed in suits and had weapons. We later learned we would be traveling with security guards, both on the bus and in cars leading and following the bus. They would continue with us for the remainder of our time in Russia.

We arrived at the hotel and were given our room assignments and told there would be a happy hour in the lobby later that afternoon if we wished to participate. James and I had separate rooms. We had heard that the rooms would be a little small, so we weren't expecting too much. Our rooms were next to each other; I walked into my room and was taken aback at how large it was. It had a long hallway with a half-bath and then a large living area. This led to a large master suite and bath that was surprisingly spacious. I was certain that a mistake had been made. I went next door to see James' room, which turned out to be the exact mirror image of my room. We weren't sure how we were so fortunate to both receive such grand treatment but we decided to just enjoy our circumstances before someone let us know a mistake had been made.

After cleaning up and changing our clothes for the evening, we went down to the happy hour arranged for our group. As our other travel companions began to arrive, every one of them was commenting about how small their rooms were and how difficult it was to maneuver around the bed and luggage to the very small bathroom. James and I said nothing and later confirmed we would never let anyone see our rooms or let them know how fortunate we were with our spacious accommodations.

We spent three days in St. Petersburg, participating in a number of private tours that included the Hermitage Museum, the Church of the

Savior of Spilled Blood, the Peterhof Palace and Garden, and Catherine Palace and Park. It was at the Catherine Palace where we were treated to a unique and beautiful experience. From our bus, we were provided open carriages for a sunset tour of the grounds before going inside the palace for a private tour and dinner. The park and palace were closed to the public at this time, so we were the only people on the grounds. At the end of our tour of the palace, we gathered in the ornate ballroom and were greeted by a dance group, dressed in period costumes that performed for us during the cocktail hour. We were later taken to a dining area for a superb seated dinner in an indescribably beautiful setting. Before leaving for the evening, we were brought outside to a large balcony overlooking the main court and were presented with a parade of riders and horses all decorated in colorful dress, creating the perfect ending to an amazing tour and dinner experience, the likes of which we had never experienced before.

The next morning, we left the hotel to board the river barge on the Volga River for our three-stop tour with the RNO. We were assigned two rooms due to their small size. One room was to be designated for luggage and the other for sleeping. Each had a very small bathroom, so we didn't have to share the space when getting ready to leave the boat or prepare for bed at night. The RNO and our group were the only people on the barge, which provided us with more space to roam around the common areas, as well as a dining area large enough for all of us to be on the same meal schedule. For each of the three stops on tour, there was an organized excursion for our group while the orchestra members went to the concert venue for a rehearsal. These were fairly small towns, but they provided us with a variety of activities mostly centered on their local culture.

Each evening, when we arrived at the concert hall, there would be a private cocktail reception for our group. It was impressive how each town had a beautifully designed venue with amazing acoustics that was large enough to accommodate the orchestra and all the patrons. Each concert was sold out, and the audience members were warm and welcoming to our group. After the concert, a local group of dignitaries would host a reception for our group and a few special guests and dignitaries from the area. The river cruise continued without a hitch; we enjoyed each town we visited and the various ways they presented their local cultures. The orchestra was doing well and enjoying adulation with each performance. We were sorry to see this part of the trip come to an end, but we were looking forward to visiting Moscow.

The hotel in Moscow was beautiful and definitely more enjoyable for all of our group members. It was a newer hotel with spacious rooms and bathrooms large enough for us to share. There were organized tours for our group throughout the city, including the Kremlin, St. Basil's Cathedral, Red Square, GUM department store, and the Arbat Street shopping area. But the two highlights of this trip were yet to come. The first was a concert with the RNO performing Gordon Getty's composition entitled Joan and the Bells. This was one of the centerpieces of this trip, and if I remember correctly, it was the first time it was being performed in Russia. The concert was held in a beautiful hall with pre- and post-concert receptions for our group. Because we were now in a major city, there was no limit to the quality level of catering and drinks at the receptions. We were all dressed in black-tie, which enhanced the magic of this evening of entertainment and hospitality.

On our last day in Moscow, we traveled by bus to the Tchaikovsky House Museum for a private tour and luncheon. Mikhail Pletnev who is RNO's founder and conductor joined us. He wanted to celebrate the ending of our amazing experience in Russia. After our tour of the museum and lovely luncheon outside in the garden, we were brought back into the home for a special treat. We were seated in the living room, and Pletnev announced that he would perform The Seasons on Tchaikovsky's personal piano (Pletnev, by the way, is the Gold Medal and First Prize winner of the 1978 Tchaikovsky International Piano Competition). We had no idea he had this special performance planned for our farewell, and to listen to him perform in Tchaikovsky's private home was unimaginable. We never could have dreamed of this opportunity; it is forever ingrained in my memory.

We could not have planned a more perfect trip and really did not want it to end, but flying home on a private jet took some of the pain away. This time, we stopped at the airport in Gander, Newfoundland, to refuel. This was a desolate area that looked like it didn't see much activity, so it was suggested that we stay on the plane. Little did we know that this place would host over seven thousand stranded travelers when all airplanes were grounded after the 9/11 attacks, inspiring the hit Broadway musical Come from Away. When many years later I saw the play, the memories from this trip came rushing back and brought a huge smile to my face as I reflected on all of the wonderful things we did on this trip.

The Concorde

Going on a cruise was James' and my favorite form of travel. Over the years, we went on more than a dozen trips that varied from the Caribbean to the Panama Canal, to a river barge on the Elbe River from Prague to Berlin. Our favorite cruise was usually on Cunard's QE II and most frequently the Atlantic Crossing between NYC and London. The trip that stands out the most for me was a round-trip package in 2000 that Cunard created with British Airlines to take the Concorde (a turbo-jet-powered supersonic passenger plane) from NYC to London and return to NYC on the QE II. We only did this once, and it was an unforgettable experience. It began with arriving at the Concorde's lounge at Kennedy airport, which was beautifully decorated and had unlimited drinks and food that were beyond anything we'd ever seen. Everything was first class, and with only about one hundred passengers, very spacious and comfortable. Eventually, we were directed to board the plane. Once you step in and look down the single-aisle with a two-two seating configuration, you know you are in for a unique travel experience. The cabin is very small compared to other commercial planes, with a low ceiling and very small circular windows. We located our seats and, while waiting for the other passengers to board, began reading the literature we were given about the plane to prepare us for the flight. The literature informed us that this plane had a maximum speed over twice the speed of sound, at 1,354 mph. It flies at 60,000 feet with an average cruising speed of 1,300 mph, making the flight to London a little over three hours.

While taxiing to our designated runway, we were informed about what was about to happen during takeoff, but I don't think you could ever be prepared because the Concorde is like no other plane. When the engines approached full power, the sound was almost deafening. We began our ascent immediately. We were all waiting for that moment when the engines were pushed to the point where we would approach the speed of sound (767 mph). As we were forced back into our seats, we heard the sonic boom. As we reached cruising speed, the sound of the engines was still loud, but it was comfortable. The attendants began serving refreshments, starting with the endless stream of champagne. At one point, I looked out the window and was surprised that at 60,000 feet, you can see the curvature of the earth and are well above the cloud level, so the view is completely unobstructed. The service was non-stop, with amazing food. Before we knew it, we were beginning our descent into London. I knew this would most likely be a one-time experience, so I soaked up every moment and was pleased to receive a document verifying that we'd been on the trip. After a few days of visiting London, we took a private car down to Southampton to board the QE II for the return trip to NYC. As much as we enjoyed being on the ship again, the Concorde experience was the definite highlight of this trip.

Irish Georgian Society I, II, & III

In 1991 we received a phone call from two friends in Dallas proposing that we join them in forming an American support group for the Irish Georgian Society (IGS). We had traveled with these friends a number of times. The purpose of the IGS is to promote awareness and the protection of Ireland's architectural heritage and decorative arts. Our Dallas friends had been in contact with the founder, Desmond Guinness, and were planning a special trip to Paris with private tours, dinners, luncheons, and cocktail parties, creating a tour so unique one could never plan it on their own. Joining this group would require a separate and sizable donation to the IGS and would be limited to twenty participants. Our friends shared with us the dates, some of the planned activities, and the total cost of the trip. We had to provide our own transportation to and from Paris, but everything else would be included. After a few days of deliberation, we called back to say we would love to join them and looked forward to the trip. We would end up going on three trips with this group—to Paris, Italy, and Ireland.

I: Paris

We arrived in Paris and went to the host hotel, which was Hotel Plaza Athenee. WOW! This is a beautiful hotel in a great location that has everything one could ever want or need. If the beauty and opulence of this hotel were any indication, we were in store for a truly magnificent experience. One of our Dallas friends had an apartment in Paris, and our group went there for an opening reception and to meet the other participants as well as some of the hosts for our trip's planned activities. The apartment was beautiful, in a great location, and when you stepped onto the balcony off the living room, you had an amazing view of the Eiffel Tower. What a great way to begin a week of extraordinary luncheons, dinners, receptions, and tours of the region surrounding Paris. Two of the luncheons and dinners stand out among all the others.

The first luncheon was at a family country estate on the outskirts of Paris. The hosts were the Marc Porthault family of the exclusive D. Porthault luxury linen company. I was not familiar with their linens, but apparently, they are well known worldwide, as I would soon find out. The setting of their home was beautiful, and the gardens were lush and colorful. The family could not have been more gracious and the food more delicious. We were seated outside at one long table, and the person across from me was the son, who was very friendly and entertaining. He was closer to my age than most of the people in our group, and we quickly bonded and had a great time. During the luncheon, I noticed how beautiful the linens were and how the countryside design decorated with pheasants would make a wonderful wedding present for my brother. He was an avid hunter and getting married the following spring. I asked Marc's wife about the pattern and if it was still available for purchase in one of their shops. She said it was and that they had a shop near our hotel where I could order a set of placemats and napkins. She also said she would write a note for me to give to the manager, and I would get the "family discount." I was not expecting such a generous offer but gratefully accepted it. Before we left to return to the hotel, their son said he wanted to show me around and gave me a tour of their beautiful home along with the surrounding gardens. I almost did not want to leave, but our trip was only just beginning.

The next day, James and I went down the street to the Porthaults' shop. I'm not sure what the note said, but when we went in, the manager could not have been more accommodating, and I truly felt we were receiving the red carpet treatment. I ordered a set of four placemats and napkins. When I received the bill of sale, I could not have appreciated the family discount more, because these linens are really expensive. The wedding wasn't for another six months, but I couldn't wait to see my brother's reaction when he opened this gift, and I could tell him the story about how it was purchased. On a side note, about a week before the wedding, the linens still had not arrived. I finally called the shop in Paris to inquire about the status of the order and was promised it would arrive in time. The package did arrive, but only the day before we were leaving town, six months after placing the order.

The other luncheon highlight was again in the countryside on the outskirts of Paris. We soon learned that the owner of this house was Mick Jagger! Yes, that Mick Jagger of the Rolling Stones. Desmond's mother had lived in Paris and knew Mick and a lot of people from all walks of life. The only downside was that Mick was not in residence at this time, but he made sure we would have an incredible lunch. We were able to freely walk throughout the house, and I tried my hardest to find something that said "Mick" where I could take a photo to prove to people where I was. But I couldn't find anything—not so much as a concert poster or painting. But in the last room, I went in, there was a small caricature of Mick on the mantel, and I made sure James took a photo so I would have my souvenir.

It wasn't a large house, but it was on sizable property with gardens and a series of grottos or shallow caves along the back. Inside each of these was a different food or beverage station where we could roam and prepare a plate. The food was really good, and the setting was beautiful. The fact that all of this had been prepared especially for our group, made it feel truly special.

For dinner one night, we were asked to dress in black-tie and meet in the lobby around 6:00 p.m. to board the bus. As we drove out of the city, we were able to view some of the city's most beautiful landmarks as the sun was setting. When we arrived at our destination, the sun had already set, and it was completely dark and difficult to see anything. As we departed the bus, the driver and an assistant had flashlights to help guide us to a walkway that headed down to a large home, maybe a castle that had numerous candles along the front banister. The building was some distance away, so we had time to adjust our eyes to the dark, and eventually, we could make out our destination. It truly qualified as a castle. About halfway down, we could hear horns playing beautiful music. They sounded like French horns, and sure enough, out of the darkness appeared twelve musicians dressed in beautiful costumes who began leading us for the remainder of the walk down to our destination. When we finally arrived on the front balcony, we entered a huge great room, two stories high with a large staircase on the other side. The musicians gathered on one side of the room and continued playing as our host couple descended the staircase to welcome us. It turned out that the owners of this home had been called out of town at the last minute, and this couple was standing in for them. After a few words of welcome, we followed them up the staircase to a cocktail reception, where a group of locals was already gathered. We were in what was called the ballroom;

it was very elegant with large mirrors and beautiful decor. We mingled with the assembled group and had a wonderful time. Later on, we were directed back downstairs to the dining room.

It was one large room with a long table set beautifully with china, crystal, flowers, and silver for forty people. James and I were impressed they had matching dinner service for forty and that the room was large enough to set up one large table that extended from one end of the room to the other. Since we were such a large group, we were instructed to sit anywhere we pleased rather than attempting an assigned seating arrangement. Looking around, we were impressed with how beautiful the room was, with exquisite architectural details, gilding, and decor. We remained at the table for about three hours of endless champagne and wine, a delicious dinner, and impeccable service. If we were going to keep up this rich diet of French food, we would need to do more walking around the city for the needed exercise, but we were definitely going to keep enjoying it all.

For our last night in Paris with our group, we were invited to another private residence for dinner. But this time, our destination lay within the city limits, and James and I knew the hostess, as she was an American from Texas and NYC. We were to arrive by 7:00 p.m., but Desmond wanted us to stop by a friend's home for a drink before dinner, so we gathered at 5:30 in the lobby. We arrived at our first destination around 6:00, and Desmond assured us we would only stay for a drink and leave. But with Desmond's charm and the gift of gab, we didn't leave until about 7:15, making our dinner arrival after 8:00 p.m. We were sure Desmond had called our host and arranged for our late arrival but were horrified and embarrassed to find out he had not. When we did arrive, our host was livid. She told Desmond she was sure our dinner would be ruined. She had planned for us to have a drink first so we could mingle with the other guests before dinner.

Eventually, she cooled down and began to enjoy the evening. After some mingling, she invited us downstairs for dinner. We were directed into a large room with an indoor pool in the center. A large number of tables for six or eight were scattered around the pool and beautifully set with gorgeous flower arrangements. Wall sconces and candles provided subdued lighting that reflected beautifully off the water in the pool. We sat down to another delicious dinner with lovely background music and enjoyed another wonderful Parisian experience. Though there had been plenty of alcohol consumed during the evening, no one fell into the pool, something James and I were sure would happen.

We planned to stay an extra day in Paris to make sure we had seen everything we wanted to and to do a little shopping. We couldn't resist doing something considered a little touristy and booked dinner on one of the famed river cruises on the Seine. It actually was very enjoyable, and we were glad we did it, as it was a nice way to end our incredible trip with something just for the two of us.

II: Italy

A few years later, we received another call from our Dallas friends, who were planning another trip for the IGS; this time, they were going to Italy. Since James and I loved traveling in Italy, and they were planning on visiting cities we hadn't been to, we immediately signed up to join the group. The trip began in Venice and would end in Milan eight days later. Desmond Guinness was with us on the trip, and again, he took us to some beautiful private homes for amazing receptions, luncheons, and dinners hosted by friends of his. The level of hospitality of our hosts and the incredible food only got better with each visit.

A favorite memory from the trip is from after our three-day tour of Venice, when we traveled to Vicenza and Piacenza, where we were to be hosted for a number of activities by a most delightful family of five brothers and their families. We learned that the grandfather had built a very large and successful business that consisted of five independent companies. When he died, he gave a company to each of his five sons, who then continued to be very successful in their own right. Though each of the families invited us to their magnificent homes for incredible events, two stand out for being exceptional experiences. On our first night, we went for dinner to a beautiful home where we began with cocktails on the main floor and were introduced to various members from each of the five families and other guests. Together with our group, there were around one hundred people. After a while, we were directed downstairs to a special dining area that resembled a cavern, with walls that were finished in stucco and curved up to a beautifully designed ceiling. There were ten tables with assigned seating, and it took a little time for everyone to get settled. We enjoyed looking around the beautifully designed and lighted room with the tables covered in gorgeous flowers and tableware. Many courses of delicious food were brought out during the evening, with endless servings of champagne and wine. What James and I admired most was how this family had planned for each of them to move from table to table throughout the dinner so they could visit with each person in our group; in turn, we were able to get to know each of them. This friendly gesture left a wonderful impression on us that continued throughout our remaining time in this region.

On our last day with this family, we were invited to one of their country estates for an outdoor luncheon in a beautiful setting overlooking the gorgeous countryside. By this time, we felt like we had known this family for years rather than just a few days; conversing with them was very easy, and they made us feel so welcomed. As we walked around their property, we would stop at various stations where food was being prepared on the spot from scratch. At one of the stations, the cooks were preparing something I had never seen before. They had soft shell crabs crawling around in a large basket; next to that was a boiling pot of oil. They scooped up a few of the crabs, mixed them in a bowl of seasoned breading, then placed them in the boiling oil for a few minutes before arranging them on a large platter. We were then invited to take a few to taste along with some vegetables as one of our courses. As the afternoon wore on, we visited each of the stations for one of the best lunches I had ever experienced. Before we left to return to our hotel, one of the children I had gotten to know the best wanted to show James and me around the house so we could see their art collection, a common interest we had shared in a previous conversation. What a wonderful way to end our time in this beautiful region of Italy.

Our tour ended with a three-day visit to Milan, where we had private tours throughout the city planned especially for our group. Our last night was a dinner hosted by a local family in their private home. Though all of the homes we visited were exceptionally beautiful, each one had something unique that made it even more special than the others. This home was in the city, so there was no view from what we could tell, but there was plenty of beauty on the inside, with exquisite decor throughout the house. What I really admired was their large collection of Lalique vases and colorful pieces beautifully displayed in each of the rooms. I had seen a lot of Lalique before, but never this large of a collection in one home. We later enjoyed a seated dinner that was elegantly presented in a very comfortable setting. James and I were so pleased to have been invited to join this group. It was the best trip we ever had in Italy—but it wasn't over for us just yet.

One thing we liked to do after taking a tour like this, where each day was filled with mostly non-stop and fast-paced activities, was to take a few days to ourselves and just relax. So we planned to go to Lake Como for a few days and stay at the amazing Villa d'Este. This hotel was as beautiful as I'd imagined, in a setting like few others, with amazing gardens and lake views. We checked in at the front desk, and as we turned to go to our room, we surprisingly ran into a couple we knew from Austin who'd just arrived in Italy to begin their ten-day tour. After talking for a few minutes, we said we hoped we would see them again before we left for home. We continued to our room, and though it was beautiful with a view overlooking the gardens, we were disappointed that it did not have a good lake view. Since it was fall and off-season, we were sure we could change to a room with a better view. When we inquired about moving, the manager said they only had one room left with a lake view, and she offered to show it to us. We walked in and had to stop in our tracks to take in the splendor of this room. We were standing in a large, high-ceilinged living room with two sets of French doors opening onto a large balcony overlooking the lake. Once we had acclimated ourselves to this amazing setting, we continued down a short hallway that had a large marble bath on one side and French doors on the other side, again opening onto the same large balcony. Then we entered the immense bedroom, which again had two sets of French doors opening onto the same balcony with the extraordinary view. As we walked back to the living room, I was prepared to go back to our original room, thinking the cost of this room would be too outrageous. James asked the manager for the daily rate, and when she told him—, and yes, it was outrageous—I started for the door. But I stopped short when after a moment's pause James said we would take it. I could not have been more surprised or pleased because this room was truly incredible. We later learned that this was the only room like it in the hotel.

We went down to the restaurant for dinner, and after we were seated, the waiter brought water and bread to the table and asked if we were guests of the hotel. We said yes, and told him our room number. He looked up at us and replied, "Ah, the best." We could not argue with him and enjoyed another amazing Italian dinner. We had a very relaxing few days on Lake Como with no real agenda. We walked around Como one day, looking through the various shops. Another day we took a boat across the lake to Bellagio, a beautiful resort town with lots of shops and restaurants. We went for a walking tour and then had lunch. We were so impressed with how nice everyone was, and the locals seemed to be very happy.

I was hoping an Italian friend, Luca, who lived on Lake Maggiore, would join us one day, but I never heard from him. After we arrived home, I received a letter from Luca saying he had called the hotel and asked for me, but they didn't have me listed as a guest. Only James' name was on the register, which he didn't know, so he assumed we had not made it. But on our last night, we invited our friends from Austin to join us in our room for cocktails before heading down to dinner. We had a wonderful time talking about our experiences in Italy while they told us about the tour they were going to begin the following day. We left for the airport the following morning and returned to Milan to catch our plane home. We were glad that we had taken this time to have a relaxing weekend in such a beautiful setting to end our remarkable tour of Italy.

III: Ireland

A few years later, our friends from Dallas called us to share their plans for a ten-day tour in Ireland with Desmond Guinness, beginning in Shannon and ending in Dublin. The culminating event would be the Green Silk Ball benefiting the Irish Georgian Society. It sounded like a wonderful trip, and we were available, so we decided to sign up immediately for what we were sure would be an incredible way to see the country.

We arrived at Shannon Airport and took a car to our hotel, Adare Manor. This is a beautiful hotel set on 840 acres that began as a private home built in 1720. It went through a three-decade renovation project beginning in 1820, turning it into a massive hotel with a golf course and impressive gardens. The public rooms are on a grand scale, with impeccable decor. The rooms are beautifully decorated with wonderful views of the surrounding countryside. We attended a cocktail reception with our tour group to reconnect with some people we had traveled with before and a few others who were new to our group. Dinner was presented in a private area, where we continued our conversations and caught up on what people had been doing since our last time together.

We spent a few days touring the Shannon region, visiting historic buildings, private estates, and gardens. We also went on walking tours of local villages in Limerick and Galway. We left Adare Manor a few days later to move inland and tour the southern region, including Cork, Waterford, and Wexford. Some of the highlights included touring the Waterford Crystal factory and going to a private estate known for its beautiful gardens, where we enjoyed a delicious luncheon. After two days in this region, we worked our way up toward Dublin, where we would end our tour. This was Desmond's home, and one night he hosted a dinner at his residence, Leixlip Castle, where we enjoyed roaming the surrounding gardens and public rooms. Desmond related the history of the castle and shared his favorite memories of living there. We spent the next few days walking the streets of Dublin and touring the region. For our last evening, we boarded a bus to travel toward the border of Northern Ireland to a magnificent Irish Georgian home, the site of the Green Silk Ball. We arrived shortly before sunset, so we were able to take in the magnificent views of the surrounding countryside with cocktails in hand. There were a few hundred people in attendance from all over Ireland, dressed in black-tie and beautiful gowns with spectacular jewelry. There were food stations scattered around the home and on the numerous porches and balconies. There was a ballroom with a large dance floor and band to entertain us throughout the night. My ballroom dance lessons came in handy, as there was no shortage of women who wanted to dance. Fortunately, all the doors to the outside were open, so the room stayed comfortable, and I was able to keep dancing without getting too warm. On the ride back to Dublin, we talked about our favorite parts of the trip and the possibility of seeing each other again on a future trip back in the states. We went to the airport the next morning to board our plane home, not realizing this would be the last trip we would take with the Irish Georgian Society. But there would be other trips in the future where we would see some of these people again.

Queen Mary II Cruise around South America

James frequently received brochures in the mail from a variety of cruise companies, and we took many cruises over the years. Cunard was one of our favorite companies because of its consistently high standards of service, accommodations, and entertainment. In 2007, James read a brochure about a new ship coming into service that piqued his interest, the Queen Mary II. One of their upcoming trips would be their first around-the-world cruise, which departed from Florida with the first leg being a thirty-day cruise around South America; at the end of that leg, we could disembark in Los Angeles. He was really interested in doing this and inviting a longtime friend, Jimmy, who lived in Houston, to join us because he had recently fallen on difficult times and could no longer travel like he had in the past. James thought this would be a great way to brighten his spirits. I was looking forward to the trip, but a few weeks after we signed up, I was selected to chair a fund-raiser that was scheduled for the week after we returned from the cruise. I was a little uncomfortable about being out of the country during the four weeks before the gala, uncertain whether I would be able to coordinate final details with my committee from so far away. I met with the committee and the development people who were working on this event, and we came up with a plan to make it work. I would have access to e-mails during the cruise and committed to contacting the committee at least three times a week. We also attempted to get as many of the details worked out before I left so that most of the decision-making would be done. With this plan in place, I went on with the planning for the trip and felt a little more comfortable that everything would work out.

On the day before the cruise, the three of us flew to Ft. Lauderdale so we would be near the port on the day of departure. We had dinner that night at the vacation home of friends from Austin who were in town and talked about the trip and what we were most looking forward to. We also shared cruise stories from the past, including one from the QE II, where James and Jimmy first met. The next morning we arrived at the port and were taken to our respective rooms, where Jimmy's was about eight cabins down the hall from our room. We met up about an hour later to walk around the ship to become familiar with the locations of the various public rooms and restaurants since none of us had been on this ship before. We also stopped by the main restaurant; on past cruises, we usually met with the maitre d' to pre-select our assigned dinner table. We were told to come back at the dinner hour, and we would receive our table assignment at that time. We went back to our rooms to get dressed and met up again to go to the restaurant for dinner. As we were being shown to our table, we assumed we would have a table for four and maybe be able to invite some single passengers to join us throughout the voyage. But we saw we were approaching a table for six where three female passengers were already seated. I quickly stopped the maitre d', stepping back a few feet and asking him what he was doing; we'd assumed we were getting a table to ourselves. He said this was the table we had been assigned to, and there really weren't any other options available. The three of us discussed the situation and shared the same concern that we would be with these people every night for thirty days. What if we didn't get along? In the end, we decided there was nothing to do but go to our table and hope for the best.

After we sat down, we went around the table and introduced ourselves. During dinner, we found out that two of the women were sisters from the British Isles; one was married and lived in Israel, and the other was in the financial sector and lived on one of the Shetland Islands. The other woman was a widow who had been married to a very successful man in Los Angeles who had a very prominent art museum named after him that we had toured. She was signed up for the complete around-the-world cruise while the two sisters were doing the same portion we were and would be departing in Los Angeles. We enjoyed the rest of our meal, slowly breaking the ice, and by the end of dinner concluded that this arrangement could possibly work out for the remainder of the cruise. It helped that Jimmy was a big talker and storyteller with a great sense of humor and that the financial sister had a very outgoing personality with an edge of naughtiness. It was interesting that for the remainder of the trip, we never saw any of our table mates on the ship but would only see them in the dining room for dinner every evening and rarely for breakfast or lunch. So when we did get together for dinner, we had ample opportunity to share our experiences from the day, providing us with fresh conversation material. As the trip progressed, we were also getting more comfortable and would begin sharing more personal information about each other. We ended up having a delightful time at dinner, with plenty of storytelling and laughter. I guess our dining experiences were being noticed by other passengers because numerous times, people would stop by our table and comment about how much fun we seemed to be having. Many would ask how long we had known each other since it appeared we were getting along so well. They were surprised when we told them we had just met on this trip. In the end, our dinner experiences became a highlight of the trip.

It didn't take us long to establish a routine during the daytime. It was remarkable that James was able to take two naps a day—one after breakfast and the other after lunch—and still be able to sleep soundly through the night. We enjoyed playing trivia each afternoon; we would get together with a different group each time and get to meet a lot of fun people from all over the world. While James was taking his afternoon nap, I would go down to the fitness area and attempt to work off all of the rich food we were consuming. After dinner, we would watch a movie or attend a musical show in the theatre. Before retiring to our cabin for the evening, we usually stopped by a piano bar at the end of our hallway for a drink and to listen to whoever was performing that evening. We soon befriended a waiter from Germany who would always get our drinks without asking and bring them to our table. On quieter nights, he would spend a lot of time talking to us, which made us feel at home.

We didn't do any excursions at the various ports where we docked because there wasn't anything of interest to us but we looked forward to going around the cape, which was the highlight of the trip. We did plan to disembark in Lima because the three of us shared a friend, Lucho, we knew from Houston, who was Peruvian and was now living in Lima. We had to wait for the tour groups to leave before we could disembark and were surprised at the size of the port; normally, you would step off the ship, and the gates out of the port were within an easy walking distance. This port was enormous, and we had to take a taxi to get to the main gate. When we arrived, James and Jimmy stayed in the taxi, and I went to go out the gate to see if I could find Lucho. When I tried to go through, the guard stopped me and said he was uncomfortable with me going out by myself. I explained that I was just going out to find our friend who was picking us up. He let me go through but said to stay close so he could keep an eye on me for my safety. I later found out that kidnapping was an issue at the port, and he was just watching out for me. I couldn't find

Lucho. I tried to call him but couldn't get through even though there had been no issue when I called from the states. So I called a mutual friend in Austin and asked him if he would call Lucho to find out where he was and let him know we were at the main gate. He called back to say he couldn't get through either and didn't know what else he could do. After about an hour, we decided to just go back to the ship. I continued trying to get through to Lucho, but without success. We were very upset that we couldn't make this work because we were all looking forward to seeing Lucho again and he was excited to show us around his city. We shared our experience at dinner and found out that all the tour buses left out of Gate 4, which was one of seven gates out of the port. After we returned home, we found out that this was where Lucho had been waiting because he saw all of the tour buses depart from this gate, and the guards wouldn't let him into the port to come to our ship. About ten years later, Lucho began traveling to Houston and would stop off in Austin to stay with a mutual friend. They contacted me on one of these trips, and we were able to reconnect. Because of this reunion, twelve years after the Queen Mary II trip, I would travel to Peru and meet Lucho in Lima, where he was able to duplicate the day he had planned for us so many years before.

The rest of the cruise was enjoyable, but after thirty days on the ship, we were ready to depart in LA and head home to finish planning the gala I was chairing.

One thing about this trip that was so special to us was that Jimmy was diagnosed with cancer that year and passed away a year later. James was so happy to have provided this wonderful trip for Jimmy, not knowing it would be the last time we would be able to spend time together.

Chapter 5

THE UNEXPECTED ROAD TO THE WHITE HOUSE

While working on my Ph.D. at the University of Texas, I had the opportunity to do an unpaid internship for the fall semester in DC with the National Education Association (NEA). In May, prior to the internship, I was invited to a weekend conference at the NEA. We took that opportunity for James to join me a few days later to search for an apartment for me during the internship period. We initially used an apartment locator service and were shown a number of nice apartments in the DC area, but none of them seemed like a good option. James would be joining me in DC every few weeks, so we needed a place both of us would enjoy. We looked up a friend who worked with the Smithsonian and shared with her the problems we were having finding a suitable apartment. She mentioned a building near Seventh and Pennsylvania she liked, and we made an appointment for a tour. This building had once been a large department store and had been recently renovated into beautiful apartments. We liked the two-bedroom plan that would be available when we needed it, and they were very accommodating about working with our schedule, so we decided to sign the lease. The apartment was fully furnished, down to the bath towels and dishes, with a choice of two decor styles. It also came with the option of a cleaning service. Though the rent was significantly higher than we'd originally planned to spend, the location was exactly what we were looking for. We planned to make the move on Labor Day weekend and looked forward to this new adventure.

James loved going on car trips and decided it would be fun to rent a car and drive with me to DC. That way, I would not be limited on what I could bring. He would return in December, renting a car and driving back with me to Texas. But on the second day of our trip to DC, James started to feel uncomfortable with all of the road construction and the number of 18-wheelers on the highway. The thought of doing this all over again in December, with the added potential for bad weather, was not appealing. On the last leg of the trip, he announced that he would not be driving back to Texas with me, but he would provide me with an airline ticket home. I asked about how I was going to get all of the stuff I'd brought with me back home on a plane, and he said we would figure that out when the time came. I sensed that this was not a topic for further discussion; I had learned that once James made a decision that was the end of it. I didn't pursue this discussion, and we enjoyed the rest of the trip.

On the third day of our road trip, we arrived in DC in beautiful weather and very little traffic, making it an easy task to get to the apartment. We began settling in. After a few hours, we decided to take a walk in the neighborhood to look for restaurants and other establishments we might want to frequent. There were two excellent restaurants nearby, one on each corner of the building, as well as a Starbucks across the street and a bookstore in the building, along with the Shakespeare Theater. Many of the Smithsonian buildings along the Mall were just a few blocks away. All in all, we couldn't have been happier with our decision to be in this location.

We had dinner that night at the 701 on the corner. It was a beautifully decorated venue with excellent food and service. We met the manager, Larry King, who would turn out to be a great asset to me as I became acclimated to the neighborhood. We ended up at this restaurant at least once every time James came for a visit, and Larry was always there to welcome us. The next night we went to the other neighborhood restaurant, Jaleo, which was very busy and didn't take reservations, which would prove to be a challenge in the future. But the food was amazing, and we enjoyed the energy in the room. We knew we would return.

James left the next day, and I went to the NEA for my first day as an intern. I wasn't sure what my days would look like, and I had only met my supervisor (Bob) a few times, so I was a little apprehensive. As I approached the front desk in the lobby, I was surprised about the level of security for gaining access. Every visitor had to sign in and wait for someone from your department to come and get you. Later I would be assigned a badge that would allow me access on my own. A young woman from Bob's division came down to get me and said she would be helping me get started with my assignment and learn the computer system I would need to access on a regular basis. Bob was out of the office for the next two weeks, and he'd left me a lot of information to review. I was to make use of the assistant to become familiar with the division so that when he returned, I would be fully acclimated and ready to begin working with him. I was pretty uncomfortable with starting the internship under these conditions but did my best to not be a nuisance. Over the next week, I met a lot of the staff that were very friendly and did what they could to make sure I was doing well. It was apparent that Bob was highly regarded, and the fact that he had chosen me as his intern seemed to grant me some credibility with his cohorts. As I completed the first two weeks at the NEA, I became increasingly more comfortable and looked forward to Bob's return to learn what projects I would begin working on.

I quickly developed some routines as I got used to finding my way around the city. The subway system was easy to learn and was conveniently located within two blocks of my apartment and the NEA offices. I also found a gym located a few blocks from the NEA, where I already had a membership, which I used each day after work. On the weekends, I would go to the nice gym and pool in my building. I also used my weekends to explore all the museums, restaurants, stores, and other amenities I could easily walk to from the apartment. One thing I found interesting about living in my building was that for the first six weeks, I never saw anyone on my floor, though I knew many of the units were occupied. I soon discovered, usually while riding the elevator or going through the lobby, there were a number of well-known fellow residents. They included former secretary of state James Baker, Bettie Friedan, Janet Reno, and actress Jane Alexander. But the one that I found to be most interesting happened to live on my floor. As a matter of fact, he was my next-door neighbor.

I discovered this one weekend when two of my sisters were visiting from Minnesota. They had never been to DC before, so they took the opportunity of my internship to visit for a long weekend. By the time they arrived, I had lived there for two months and was familiar enough with the city that I could give them great advice on what to see and do while I was at work. On the weekend, we went to many of the museums and important buildings throughout the city but also took advantage of some social activities. It was Halloween weekend, so we went to a large dance venue where many of the occupants were dressed in flamboyant costumes. Two of my friends (who were both over six feet tall) were there with two other friends, all of whom were dressed as Hooters girls, in full makeup and wearing roller skates, making them even more statuesque. This is not how I wanted my sisters to meet these guys, but it was a memorable experience. We stayed for many hours because the music was great and the attendees very entertaining. We had never seen anything like it before.

On another night, we went to Jaleo for dinner and wanted to have paella, which is what the restaurant was most famous for, and my sisters had never eaten it before. We started with drinks and a few tapas, but it seemed like a lot of time had passed without getting our entree. After we inquired, the manager came over and apologized profusely, saying that there had been a mix-up in the kitchen and our order had never been prepared. He said it took quite a while to make the dish and asked if he could provide us with a substitute at his expense. We explained that we had never had paella and that they were leaving the next day, so we really wanted to stay with our original order. He said he completely understood and would do his best to get us the paella as quickly as possible. In the meantime, he said he wanted to send over some of his favorite tapas for us to try—on the house. Throughout the evening, the manager frequently returned to our table. We learned that he was the owner, and his name was José Ramón. At one point, I told him I lived in the building and really enjoyed his restaurant. He replied that he too lived in the building, and when I said I lived on the tenth floor, he said he also lived on that floor. We discovered the manager lived just a few doors down from me, though I had never seen him up there. I also mentioned how difficult it was to get into the restaurant, and he told me he had a way to remedy that. He said anytime I wanted a table to come down to the host stand around 6:00 p.m., let them know what I needed, and leave my phone number. They would call my apartment when my table was ready, and we could walk through the waiting crowd and go immediately to our table. I was reluctant about this ever working out, but I did try it a few times and was successful with each attempt.

By the time the paella finally arrived, we had already eaten so many tapas that we could only eat a small portion and had to take the rest of it home. We had planned to go to a rave party where they covered the dance floor in soapsuds, but after our lengthy dinner with way too much food, we went upstairs and collapsed.

As we were heading into the building, we saw a poster for the Shakespeare Theater's next production, which had a picture of Harry Hamlin, who was going to perform the lead in Henry V. One of my sisters (Jenny) said she had a major crush on him from his L.A. Law days and wished we could run into him so she could get his autograph. Since they were leaving the next day, we were certain this would not happen.

But the next evening, after my sisters went to the airport, I was about to unlock my door when I heard someone coming out of the apartment next to mine. I decided to stall a little, so I could finally see one person on this floor. Someone came out and after locking his door, began walking toward me. I looked up as I was entering my apartment to see that it was Harry Hamlin. I was shocked as he walked by and smiled and said hello to me. I immediately went in and called Jenny to tell her that while she was visiting, he lived right next door the whole time. She was heartbroken.

Her birthday was in a few weeks, so I decided to get a card, attach a note to it asking Harry if he would sign it for my sister, and hoped for the best after sliding it under his door. A few days later, I found the card under my door with a note from Harry. He said he normally would not do this for someone he hadn't met, but he signed it anyway. I sent the card to my other sister to present at the birthday party so Jenny would know the story behind it. Later that night, she called to thank me profusely for the gesture and told me she would treasure the card forever. I'm just as big a fan of his as Jenny is, and even today, I still have the note he wrote to me on his personal stationery.

James continued coming to DC every few weeks. We had a few friends in DC with whom we would get together. One friend, in particular, Ann, was a frequent planner for a number of social events and fund-raisers that mostly supported the arts. She made sure we were on the list for galas, dinners, and receptions that were held in some of DC's most beautiful buildings, including the State Department, the Kennedy Center, Blair House, the Library of Congress, various embassies, and the White House. It was always a special treat to be invited to an event at the White House, which we did about a dozen times during the Bill Clinton and George W. Bush administrations. These included luncheons and brunches, cocktail receptions, and both buffets and seated dinners.

One opportunity that was incredibly special was when we were invited to join an organization called the Domingo Circle, established to support Placido Domingo becoming the new director of the Washington Opera. The purpose of this organization was to help financially support Domingo's position for four years and, in turn, be invited to an annual opera gala that each time occurred over a long weekend. Each gala weekend included luncheons and receptions in embassies or ambassador residences as well as a gala dinner and a performance at Kennedy Center, a White House event, and a unique dinner experience the night of the gala. The actual gala was always the last evening of the weekend, and guests would receive a dinner invitation to a specific embassy. All participants would go to one embassy for dessert and dancing. We had dinners at the Canadian Embassy, the British Embassy, and the Spanish Embassy, but the dinner that stood out the most was at the Ambassador Residence for South Korea.

It is a beautiful building with many lush gardens and exquisite decor. We had cocktails when we arrived and were introduced to the ambassador and his wife along with the other guests. At one point, we were directed to a long dinner table, low to the ground and beautifully set for twenty-four people. What I immediately noticed was the beautiful sterling silver chopsticks set with various colored stones. James and I were seated at one end of the table with the ambassador's wife between us. There were a few smaller bowls pre-set at each place setting, and I soon figured out we were having a sushi dinner. Unfortunately, sushi was something James and I never ate, and I wondered how he was going to react, especially considering who was seated between us. I think our dinner companion sensed our uncertainty as to how to approach the meal once they began serving the food. She graciously explained what everything was and recommended which sauces to use with each serving of the various types of seafood. It wasn't as bad as I thought, but I still did not become a fan of sushi and haven't had it since, though, without our companion's assistance, we wouldn't have eaten as much as we did. It was a very lovely evening, but we looked forward to going to the gala embassy to feast on the desserts. And we were not disappointed. The remainder of the gala was held at the Belgian Embassy, and we were quite pleased with the selection of desserts. They created a large table with beautiful flower arrangements made completely from chocolate, and the table was covered with almost every imaginable selection of chocolate candy. We had another enjoyable gala weekend and looked forward to these each year. We were very sorry to see them end four years later.

My time in DC was quickly coming to an end, and I was not looking forward to leaving. With the NEA, I had traveled to Florida for a national conference. I helped coordinate and visit a charter school site in California that was part of a study that was a primary focus of my responsibilities at the association. I was also able to gather and create a lot of resources for the dissertation I was going to complete when I returned to Austin. On the last day, my supervisor and staff from his department hosted a lovely going-away party for me that was very emotional and made it even more difficult for me to say goodbye.

Back at my apartment, I finished packing most of my belongings to ship home and was surprised to see that it totaled over thirty boxes. I thought I would be able to pack the remaining items in two large suitcases to take on the plane with me, but I soon realized I was not going to accomplish this. I ended up going to a street vendor to buy some duffel bags to complete my packing and ended up with seven pieces of luggage. I wasn't sure what would happen at the airport, and when I went to check my bags, the agent said there was no way I could bring all of this luggage on the plane. Though I explained that I was leaving DC for good to return home, he would not relent. When he saw that my ticket was stamped as first-class, he said this made a difference and allowed me to check in all of my baggage. Much relieved, I thanked him, tipped him generously, and went on my way to board the plane home.

I arrived in DC for my internship with no expectations of what I would experience. I really enjoyed living in the city and making many friends, saw a lot of wonderful places, and amassed a lot of information for my dissertation. I was sad to leave but looked forward to going home and being reunited with James.

Chapter 6

AN EVENING WITH ELTON JOHN, AND OTHER UNIQUE EXPERIENCES

As the population of Austin grew, so did the opportunities to attend some wonderful parties and events. A new one for us was attending Andy Roddick's gala for his foundation. He had recently moved to Austin and would rotate his gala between Austin one year and Florida the next. I attended the first gala for Andy's foundation when a friend called to invite me because she purchased a table and her husband had to suddenly go out of town, and she needed an escort. James and I had heard about the gala, but we were too late as it was completely sold out, so I was very happy to accept. I arranged for a private car and driver to take us, and when I picked her up at her home, she was ready with champagne and glasses in hand, and we were off to the party in style. Andy was a big celebrity for Austin as well as the rest of the state, so he had attendees from all over the area as well as some of his tennis buddies and a scattering of Olympic athletes. But the big draw was that he managed to get Elton John to attend. Not only would he be part of the dinner and auction, but he would also perform a private concert for the group. Elton made himself completely accessible, so many people were taking pictures or getting autographs throughout the evening with him as well as with other notable guests, such as the Olympic athletes.

The evening began with a cocktail party in the lobby of the ballroom, which flowed outside to the adjoining patio. Between my friend and me, we knew a lot of the people attending and had a great time mingling with everyone and talking about how excited we were to be there; this fundraiser was unique because of the celebrity status it held. Eventually, we were directed into the ballroom to be seated at our assigned tables to get ready for dinner. Andy got on stage a little later to welcome everyone and talk a little bit about his foundation for kids and what impact it would have on the Austin communities that were more disadvantaged and weren't able to provide sports opportunities for their children. He was an exceptional speaker and easily convinced the crowd that this was for a good cause that would directly impact our city. This led us to the live auction. There were some incredible items, including trips to tennis tournaments, stays at vacation homes, and other amazing items that Austin was not accustomed to seeing at other local fund-raisers. He was able to raise a huge amount of money in a very short time and raised the bar for any other Austin organization trying to fundraise from this community. Elton had been sitting at Andy's table the entire evening and was heavily involved in the auction, bidding extraordinary amounts; this encouraged many others to join in. At one point, he needed to prepare for his concert, so we had a break from the auction. This gave another opportunity for people to mingle and take pictures with the athletes before the lights dimmed for Elton's performance. Since this ballroom was not that large, the concert portion of the evening was very intimate, with only Elton and his piano. He performed an amazing program of his biggest hits, making this evening one of the most special ones I had ever had in Austin.

A few years later, James and I made sure we got a table for Andy's next gala and continued going for at least three more galas. One year we bid on and won a tennis package for a trip to California to attend a tennis tournament to watch Andy compete. It was a VIP experience with dinners, swag bags, photo opportunities with the players, and attendance at a press conference with Andy after one of the matches. James' granddaughter lived near where the tournament was held, and they allowed us to invite her and her mother for one of the evening pre-dinners and matches to see Andy compete and meet him after the match. The auction package also included a tennis racket autographed by Andy, which James presented to his granddaughter as a memento of the evening. This unique experience provided a wonderful opportunity to not only support Andy's foundation but also create a memorable time with family.

Another party in Austin that stood out was a fiftieth birthday party for a friend of ours. It was held at a private venue downtown that had security to ensure only invited guests could get in. There was a large two-story outdoor space lined with bars and tables of appetizers, along with an interior entertainment area large enough for more bars, food tables, and a dance floor. During the cocktail reception, we heard people talking about the possibility of a huge entertainer performing and speculating as to who it would be. The band performing that night was Grupo Fantasma, a local favorite now performing all over the country. James found a stool to sit on, and I moved closer to the stage to watch for this potential superstar. It took me a while before I saw it, but a band member came out later during one of the numbers and joined the group. I could not believe who I was looking at. It was Prince! Yes, that Prince. He just walked on stage and began playing with the group, and blended in without any special announcement. Though I am from Minnesota and lived in the same city as he did, I had never seen him perform before and was beside myself with excitement. He was only about eight feet away from me. The stage was not that high, so he was almost at eye level with me. And yes, he was VERY petite but still an amazing performer. It wasn't until later in the evening, after the band had left the stage, that he performed a few solo numbers, which was all I needed to be completely happy and satisfied. When would this ever happen again? I was in awe. Then the magic was over. He left the stage, and the band returned to complete their performance.

It was later that evening when I found out that Prince had taken a special interest in Grupo Fantasma and had hired them as the backup band for some of his concerts at his venue in Vegas. Through this relationship, our friend was able to get him to join the group for her party. This was a big deal for Austin, and a few days later, it was written up in the newspaper. This definitely was not your ordinary birthday party. The night continued on after the concert with more music, dancing, and cake to make this one amazing night in Austin.

James and I helped create a special event in Austin in collaboration with our travel agent in NYC, Susan. We belonged to a travel group that supported the American Museum in Britain, and Susan would organize fund-raising trips for the museum called Insider Tours. These tours were usually four- to five-day trips to a specific town where we would visit private homes and collections along with local museums, performing arts venues, local buildings to look at architecture unique to the area, and other venues of interest. Some of the trips we'd previously gone on included the cities of San Francisco, Washington, DC, and Minneapolis. It was on the Minneapolis trip that James asked Susan if she'd ever considered making a trip to Austin. If so, he said, we would help organize it. I was hoping she would decline the invitation; compared to what we'd experienced on past tours, I wasn't sure Austin had enough to offer, especially in art, to interest the people who go on these trips. Susan said she would consider it and contact some of her regular travelers to see if there was an interest. Another reason I was against this idea was that I knew I would be the one organizing the trip. Would I be able to secure enough private collections and public places to make it a worthwhile and interesting experience for the participants? About six weeks later, Susan called us to say she thought we should try organizing an Austin trip and gave us a week in February that worked with her schedule. We tried to get her to move it to later in the spring when we could include the wildflowers and other plants that would be in bloom, but she said it would need to be February.

We had about two months to put together an itinerary so she could prepare a brochure to advertise the trip to Austin. I began with visiting the directors of Austin's Museum of Art and the Blanton Art Museum at the university to get ideas from them as to who had the best private art collections in town and also which public spaces I should include. As for private art collections, they came up with very similar lists, which we narrowed down to about ten collections. Fortunately, through our involvement in the museums, James and I knew all of the owners, so I felt comfortable contacting them. Then I created a list of public spaces and a few homes of significant architectural or historic interest. The last list was of possible places for lunch or dinner that could accommodate a group of about twenty people. Once I had these lists completed, I had to create an itinerary that grouped the places into convenient morning and afternoon tours over four days where we wouldn't be spending a lot of time on the road traveling from place to place. Once that was finished, it was time to contact everyone to secure commitments on their designated day and time. It took a couple of days to complete this task, but luckily everyone on the list was agreeable to the schedule, making my job a lot easier than I'd imagined.

I contacted Susan with the itinerary and found out I also needed to create some sort of description of all the places we would visit so she could create the finished brochure for the attendees. This was harder than I thought, but I was able to get most of the information I needed from the internet. After a few more days, my responsibility was over, and I could prepare myself for the upcoming tour. It was during this waiting period that I decided James and I should travel in our car ahead of the tour bus to make sure everyone was ready for our group's arrival. We also planned to have our friend Bob, a local tour guide, ride on the bus and point out various landmarks the group would see while traveling through town and answer any questions people might have about our city. Susan was enthusiastic about this plan, which would make her job a lot easier.

The first day of the tour was strictly to allow time for the attendees to arrive in Austin and go to their host hotel, which Susan had set up. A welcome dinner was planned that night at the hotel, which began with a cocktail reception so we could meet and welcome everyone in the group. James and I had been on many of these trips, including the very first Insider Tour, so we knew quite a few people in the group. We introduced Bob to the group so they would know who he was and what role he would be playing on the tour. Setting up this dinner for the group was a great way to kick off the tour.

I planned the first stop of the tour to see our friend's magnificent collection of art, sculpture, and jade in their beautiful home in a historic part of town. They had built an addition to their home just to showcase their collection and really enjoyed sharing it with groups they knew were interested and would appreciate their works of art. I found out from Bob that when the group was back on the bus, they indicated that they were very impressed with what they'd seen and were very surprised that a private collection of that magnitude was in Austin. We only had to go around the block to the next stop, which was a very significant historic home named the Pease Mansion, one of Austin's best-known landmarks. I was lucky enough to run into a friend at a party about a month previously who knew the owners and helped me to secure a tour of this home. This pre–Civil War home was completed in 1853 and designed in a Greek Revival style by Abner Cook. The couple that lived there now had spent many years restoring the house to its original grandeur. When they bought the house, it was in terrible disrepair due to years of neglect. The wife was our guide, and she did a wonderful job of describing the history of the home as well as what they had to go through to get the house back to its magnificent glory. We went to lunch after these two stops. The group was very complimentary about what they had seen on just the first morning and wondered what else I had in store for them.

Over the next few days, we visited a number of private homes to see their collections as well as some public spaces like the Lady Bird Johnson Wildflower Center, which thankfully happened to have a small patch of bluebonnets in bloom. A particular highlight was a visit to a local artist's home. His work was displayed at both of the Austin art museums we toured, and I had made sure the curators pointed out his paintings. That afternoon we went to his house to meet him. He showed us his art collection plus some new pieces on which he was currently working. He also talked about some of his work on display in the states; a number of people in the group had actually seen some of this work and were very pleased to meet him. He also did an incredible demonstration of the process he went through to create specific colors. As an example, he had an orchid in his studio that was an unusual shade of purple; he showed us how he mixed a variety of paint colors to create that specific color. It was truly remarkable, and no one in our group had ever seen a demonstration like that. Few had ever visited an artist's private studio.

Another memorable experience on this tour happened while we were at lunch at the University Club before our tour of the LBJ Library. I had tried for weeks to get a commitment from Luci Johnson, a friend of ours, to see if she could join us for the tour of the library. I hadn't heard back from her, so I never said anything to anyone in the group. As we were finishing our lunch, someone came up behind me and placed their hands over my eyes, and said, "Guess who?" I turned, and there was Luci, who seemed very pleased with herself for surprising me this way. I got up and introduced her to the group, who seemed equally surprised to see her. She said a few words to welcome everyone to Austin and was excited to go on tour with us to her father's library. She met us in the library's lobby, and we went up to the top floor, where there were four large photos of public rooms in the White House as well as a replica of LBJ's Oval Office. Luci went from photo to photo, telling us wonderful stories about each of the rooms from when she was a young girl living in the White House. When we finished with the photos and Oval Office replica, Luci took us into a private apartment that was usually not open to the public. It was filled with artifacts and gifts the Johnsons had received from their time in the White House. As we walked around the apartment, she pointed out some of the artifacts that had a special meaning to her and then asked us to sit down so she could share some stories about her father. Luci is a great storyteller and was keeping all of us entertained, but what truly piqued everyone's interest was when she began talking about the day Kennedy was shot and how she found out about it. She talked about how she spent countless hours in fear, not knowing if her parents were OK or what had happened to them. She also shared about the transition to the White House and how Johnson wanted to make sure the Kennedy family had ample time to grieve and not create more upheaval in their lives. Against the advice of the Secret Service, he let them remain in the White House as long as they needed. These were all stories I had never heard before, and from the attentiveness of the group members, I'm guessing they hadn't heard such a remarkable true-life account of that time in American history.

When we got back to the bus, we told the group we had to host a table at an event that evening and would not be able to join them for the farewell dinner that night, but our friend Bob would fill in as host. They thanked us for putting together such a wonderful tour, informing us that because of this last-minute surprise visitor, we were the current winners of the Best Insider Tour Award.

Another opportunity for a unique experience brought us to NYC. Through our membership with a few history-related organizations, we had become friends with Kip Forbes from the successful publishing empire family. He sent us an invitation to attend a fund-raiser for one of these organizations (American Friends of English Heritage) on his private yacht, The Highlander, and tour the Hudson and East Rivers. We had never been on The Highlander before, so it wasn't too difficult to accept this special invitation, which also provided us with a few days to visit NYC and see some plays. When we arrived at the dock dressed in black-tie, we were blown away by the size of the ship, which also had a helicopter on top and a couple of speedboats on one of the decks. Kip greeted us once we boarded and encouraged us to walk throughout the yacht, as the entire ship was open for the party. This yacht was truly remarkable and beautifully finished, with large lounges on the main deck and multiple bedrooms below the deck. We walked outside onto numerous decks and were amazed by how clean everything was; there wasn't a speck of dirt on anything.

After everyone was on board, the ship left the dock and began the cruise as the sun was setting, and it was a beautiful evening. As we went back inside, I thought I recognized a couple across the room. As we got closer, I could not believe the people I was about to meet. It was none other than Joe and Katherine Jackson, the parents of the Jackson Five, and one of my favorite performers, Janet. A few young men joined our group, and we were introduced to Jermaine, who was with two of his brothers. This was an amazing treat. I had been a fan of theirs for years and never dreamed of ever meeting any of them, especially in such a personal and extraordinary setting. We frequently ran into them throughout the evening, during which the boys shared their plans for creating a Jackson reunion show in Vegas. Later that night, Jermaine asked to share our personal contact information so he could keep me up to date on their plans, as I had said I would not want to miss seeing them perform.

Later that evening, as we were sitting around one of the many tables scattered around one of the lounge areas eating dinner, we saw that Katherine was nearby but sitting alone, and we asked her to join us. She was very nice but quiet. Eventually, she warmed up to our group and was happy to share some stories about her many famous children. This was a special treat I will never forget, and I treasure the many photos Kip later sent us from the evening. Unfortunately, the Vegas reunion never happened, but I still had the wonderful memory of meeting members of the Jackson family under extraordinary conditions, and to this day, I treasure this experience.

A few years later, I was lucky enough to board The Highlander again, but this time it was in DC when I was doing my internship at the NEA. One night I met Kip for dinner, and he said his sister was doing a fund-raiser on the ship that included a cruise on the Potomac. He gave me the contact information to make a donation and get on the guest list. I called James when I got home to share the news, and he said how interesting it was that while I was having dinner on a yacht, he would be at the local Luby's cafeteria with a few friends, which didn't seem quite right. But he said to give Kip his regards and told me to have a great time and that he wished he could be there. This time, I didn't know any-one else on the ship but still had a wonderful time, especially enjoying the stunning views up and down the Potomac as the sun was setting.

We took a few cruises sponsored by the Smithsonian Institution that were exceptional due to the quality of the guides, tours, and experts, who would give very interesting lectures on the ship related to what we were doing and seeing on the trip. Two of these trips stand out because they were so well done and created exceptional memories that are still fresh in my mind today.

The first trip was a cruise from Seville, Spain, to Rio de Janeiro to study the slave trade and the impact it had on Europe versus South America. We began the trip with a few days of tours around the Seville area that were both interesting and educational. Then we boarded our ship for the cruise portion of the trip and were surprised that we could start on the Guadalquivir River in town and make our way down to the Atlantic. This was possible because our ship was smaller. The ship was beautiful and only had first-class cabins with very comfortable public areas and incredible cuisine. Our entertainment onboard consisted of attending a lecture each evening after dinner with an expert from the Smithsonian who would talk about the area we were leaving and introduce us to the region where our next port-of-call would be. We cruised from Seville to the Canary Islands and on to Dakar, Senegal, where we had a tour of the city with a focus on Gorée, an island that was a major outpost for the slave trade. Though the tours were well done with exceptional guides who were very knowledgeable about the region and its history, it was a very emotional experience to see firsthand where this happened and to hear about the awful conditions and practices that were in place at this time in history.

We continued our cruise across the Atlantic for three days and concluded our trip in Rio. We were taken to a hotel, and later met the group for dinner, where we were informed about the next two days of tours throughout the region. All of the tours were private, with local guides, and focused on the culture of the region; we visited landmarks and learned about their historical significance or their unique style of architecture. We also were provided private luncheons and dinners with local artists and musicians performing music and dances in beautiful costumes.

Our second Smithsonian cruise went from Istanbul to Athens, with a focus on the history of these two regions and how they impacted each other. This trip was planned to celebrate the completion of my dissertation for my Ph.D. at the university and would occur a week after my defense. It almost didn't happen because one of the committee members thought I needed to write an additional chapter, which would have prevented me from going on the trip. Fortunately, the committee chair didn't agree with her, so I was free to go on this cruise.

I had never been to Turkey or Greece before, so I was really looking forward to visiting these countries. Traveling with the Smithsonian made these trips so much more interesting because of the experts they brought on the trip, who were very good at explaining the history and interactions of these two regions. We began the trip with a four-day tour of Istanbul, visiting its most significant buildings and landmarks, including Sultanahmet Square, the Hagia Sophia, the Blue Mosque, Topkapi Palace, and the Grand Bazaar. We weren't comfortable heading out on our own, so we stayed with the selected tours set up for our group.

On the next leg of our trip, we cruised down the west coast of Turkey to tour many of their ancient sites. Some of our favorite tours included Ephesus, with its Roman terraced houses, the Celsus Library, and the Grand Theater. We also toured Miletus, with its ancient Hellenistic Theater, as well as Priene, Perge, Side, Kas, Myra, and Didyma. April seemed to be the perfect time of year to tour this coast as it wasn't too warm, and there were many wildflowers and plants in bloom, providing for beautiful settings wherever we went.

In the last part of our trip, we cruised through the Greek Isles and then disembarked for our three-day tour of Athens. Going there was the highlight of the trip for us because Athens had been on our list of places to see for many years. The best part of our tour was to finally see the Acropolis and its many ancient ruins, with the Parthenon being our favorite. We also toured the National Archaeological Museum and the Acropolis Museum. Because of my years on the track team in high school, I personally enjoyed visiting Olympia and seeing the Panathenaic Stadium, where we heard about its history of hosting many types of athletic competitions over the centuries. This trip was extremely well planned. The exceptional guides and lecturers, with their insights into the history and culture of the region, added a depth to this experience that we would not have appreciated on our own.

Over the course of our many years together, James and I experienced many outstanding trips and social events. In many ways, our life together was a dream come true.

Chapter 7

THE DIAGNOSIS

In the fall of 2004, when James was sixty-four, he went to see a neurologist on the recommendation of his primary care doctor due to some recent changes in James' health. James called me at work that afternoon to tell me the doctor thought he might have Parkinson's, but James would need further testing to confirm the diagnosis. We did not see this coming, as James had been very healthy, and there was no history of any significant illnesses in his family. We were unprepared for what lay ahead. I was saddened to hear the news and began to tear up while he was telling me about the appointment.

When I returned home after work, we went to dinner and talked about what had happened that day. I said I would go with him to future appointments so we both could hear the results and discuss any plans for treatment. Over the next few weeks, James went through a number of tests. After the doctor reviewed all the results, he confirmed James' diagnosis, and we started a medication regimen beginning with Sinemet. Over the next few months, the doctor recommended the addition of various medications to help aid dopamine levels and increase James' quality of life. Aside from a slight tremor in James' right hand, he didn't exhibit any symptoms. In March, James was experiencing lethargy and low blood pressure, and the doctor wanted to have him tested to make sure he hadn't had a stroke. His results came back negative for stroke and no sign of tumors, so we continued monitoring his blood pressure and frequent check-ups with the doctor.

Twice a year, James would have what was referred to as "the family meeting." His three children would come to Austin to meet with their financial advisors, accountant, lawyer, and estate administrators. I never attended these meetings because they didn't affect me, and they occurred while I was at work. When I returned home from work on the day of one of these meetings, James said they discussed me and thought it would be best for me to retire so we could spend more time together without the restrictions of my work schedule. While James was still in good shape, we could spend time traveling and work more on our philanthropy and community involvement. This was in June after school was over for the students, but I was still required to be at work. James asked if I would retire immediately. But I had just completed my second year as principal of a new school and didn't feel comfortable retiring without closure. I said I would consider it after another year of school. He wasn't too pleased with my answer, as he apparently had already made up his mind, but we discussed it further, and he agreed to give me the additional year. I only shared this decision with my assistant principal and secretary so they would have a year to decide what they wanted to do. I didn't let anyone else in the district know what I was planning until May of the next year after the required state achievement testing had been completed. Making this decision to retire made the rest of the school year a lot easier for me, knowing that the end was in sight. At the end of the year, I turned in my resignation, shared my plans with the rest of the school staff, and enjoyed a few farewell events with students and staff.

The remainder of 2005 and into 2006, James was doing well with his meds, and the doctor stated that James was still in the early stages of Parkinson's. But by the spring of 2006, James was experiencing increased tremors on his right side. Some modifications were made to his meds, which made a noticeable change. The tremors increased again in the fall, and two new meds were prescribed, which helped him improve. December and January brought a new list of issues, including pneumonia, a persistent cough, and some disorientation. Multiple doctors were brought in to provide the necessary treatments, and by the end of January, James was feeling well again.

After a routine visit with his cardiologist, it was determined that James required angioplasty to insert two stents for blocked arteries. The procedure was successful, and James didn't require any changes to his meds. During the summer, we discovered James was having tremors at night, causing him to bite his tongue and the side of his cheek while sleeping. We tried various medications, but nothing seemed to be successful. By the end of the summer, our doctor decided he had done all he could to treat James, and we should consider a new plan of treatment. In the fall of 2007, our doctor recommended another specialist who focused solely on Parkinson's patients.

During the first six months with the specialist, we had regularly scheduled appointments with the doctor along with a nutritionist and physical therapist he had in his practice. Their goals included ways to improve James' alertness, balance, and general strength while monitoring his blood pressure, as some days James would feel a little "off" and unsteady on his feet. The doctor adjusted James' medications many times, trying to strike the right balance. Some of the new meds appeared to be effective, but others had serious side effects, so I was constantly monitoring James and reporting any problems back to the doctor. By the end of the year, James was feeling much better and had very few "off" days, so we felt we finally had a good plan in place.

James remained in good health for the next six years. We didn't have to make any changes to his meds, and he demonstrated very few, if any, symptoms normally associated with Parkinson's. With James this healthy, we were able to frequently travel and to attend many local functions, concerts, and fund-raisers. We were also able to host a large number of dinner parties and community events at El Greco. Some of the more memorable parties included our twenty-fifth-anniversary party for thirty friends,

James' sixty-fifth and seventy-fifth birthday parties, and regular pool parties on Sundays throughout the summer. We were also taking annual family trips to Vegas because of some tax-related business with the estate. We usually stayed for three days at the Four Seasons above Mandalay Bay, though the family only needed to meet for a few hours and complete some paperwork. This allowed us time to see many shows, including most of the Cirque du Soleil productions, and have extraordinary dinners in some of the city's best restaurants.

Every once in a while, James would ask to do something out of the ordinary. One time James said he wanted to go to a Lady Gaga concert because he had been hearing her name mentioned a lot on TV, and he wanted to see what the fuss was all about. She was scheduled for a concert in Austin, and I was able to secure tickets for us. We rented a limo for the night, went to dinner with two friends, and arrived in time for the concert. I thought I selected tickets with an unobstructed view of the stage so James would not have to stand, but unfortunately, the section in front of us came all the way up to our row, making it difficult to watch the concert without standing. There was a large screen near us showing the performance, though, and we were able to hear everything, so we enjoyed the experience. We found out through friends that word had quickly spread around town that we'd attended this concert because few people could believe that James would want to. This was the last concert we would attend because of the difficulty of maneuvering through the crowds and accessing the seats, but it was a concert worthy of being our last one to attend.

One of the most memorable parties we attended during this time was at the invitation of an Austin friend who enjoyed hosting extravagant birthday parties in Beverly Hills. We were using a private jet service for travel within the US, and she asked us if we could fly six guests from Austin with us to the party. We made the arrangements for an upgrade to a larger plane because the jet we normally used was large enough for only six passengers. But about a week before the trip, we were called with a scheduling problem. This company was involved in a large poker tournament in Las Vegas, and the plane we were going to use would no longer be available. They told us we could use our regular plane, but what we were supposed to do with the two additional guests? They recommended we tell them they needed to fly commercial, but we said that would not be acceptable. After a long discussion, I presented a plan where four of us would fly the day before, and the remaining four passengers would fly the next day on the scheduled flight. They said they could accommodate us, so we put the plan into action and adjusted our hotel reservations to include an additional day. But we also let them know that we were very disappointed with the way this trip was handled with these last-minute changes.

We had attended a few of the past parties hosted by our friend, and they'd been spectacular. For one, the host created a rooftop lounge at the Beverly Wilshire Hotel for a concert featuring Etta James. At another, Kenny G serenaded us during a cocktail reception, and then there was a seated dinner and private concert in a highly decorated airport hangar with Hall & Oates. This time we were staying at the Montage. The first evening, there was a concert and dinner in the hotel restaurant, which had been completely transformed into a beautiful venue just for our group. The next evening was a sumptuous dinner and, again, a private concert with Hall & Oates in the hotel's ballroom. Since we had arrived a day early, our plane mates took us out to dinner at a wonderful restaurant in Beverly Hills. We ended the weekend with dinner at the Beverly Hills Hotel hosted by two other people who were flying on our private plane. After dinner, as we were waiting for our car, James whispered, "Look over there." Shaquille O'Neal was getting out of a car. I was surprised to see Shaq in person, but I was more surprised that James actually knew who he was since James was not known for having any interest in sports. We had a wonderful weekend, and the next day headed for the airport, where this time, we had a jet large enough to accommodate the total group of eight.

While we were in the private jet terminal waiting to board our plane, we watched in awe as this huge private jet was being directed near the entrance to the tarmac. One of our guests mentioned how nice it would be to travel on that jet and wondered to whom it belonged. As we continued to wait, I reached into my pocket to see what our jet's tail number was and was completely surprised to see it matched the tail number of the huge jet in front of us. When I told our travel companions, they thought I was kidding until I showed them our jet's tail number. I then told them we had obviously been given what I referred to as a "NetJet apology." The plane had a huge galley, two large lounges, and a flight attendant to provide us with anything we wanted. This surprise upgrade was to make up for the last-minute cancellation and any inconvenience. We never expected this kind of service and were truly grateful for their generous gesture. What we didn't realize at the time was that this would be our last trip with this private jet company.

James decided he wanted to host one more extraordinary event. It would be for his upcoming eightieth birthday. We began the planning process by locating a venue that would be large enough for up to three hundred guests. We narrowed our choices to two locations; our top pick was the Four Seasons; we had been there a number of times for events and knew the high level of service they were capable of providing. However, they would not allow us access to the ballroom until 3 p.m. the day of the party, which would not give us enough time to set up for what would turn out to be an epic event. So we went to the historic Driskill Hotel. We were less familiar with it but were impressed with their presentation, especially when we attended a menu-tasting meeting that exceeded our expectations. We hired an event planner to assist us in creating a party that would be talked about for years to come.

We started with the design of the save-the-date cards, beautiful place cards with a schedule for the evening, and custom-designed invitations that would become sought-after keepsakes. We met with our favorite florist, who presented us with a mixed bouquet of flowers in various shades of colors he would use for the table arrangements. Then there was the arduous task of creating the guest list and assigned seating chart for the dinner portion of the evening. The Driskill assisted us in this process by providing a floor plan that laid out how the tables would be positioned in the ballroom. James was involved in every step of the planning process, but he left me with the tasks of implementation and oversight due to the fact that I had chaired three fund-raising galas in recent years. I'm not sure we were aware of how large this event was going to be. We determined that we needed to plan flights, ground transportation, hotel accommodations, a family dinner the night before the party, and a reception and dinner at El Greco for our family members and numerous out-of-town guests the evening after the party.

A few months into the planning process, I had lunch with a friend with a lot of party-planning experience and with whom I had co-chaired a gala. After we reviewed the plans to date for what now was turning into a long weekend of activities, I said the only thing I hadn't figured out yet was the entertainment for the reception at El Greco the evening after the party. After some brainstorming, she said the obvious choice would be to get the woman who had performed at his fiftieth birthday party in Houston because he still frequently talked about her and that event. I was uneasy about this idea because that party was thirty years prior, and I was unsure if she was still performing. My friend said that this was where she could help, and she took it upon herself to locate this woman and find out if she was still performing and available. She got back to me within a few days to say she had located the performer, who was still singing and would be available for our dinner party. The event planner contacted the manager to create the contract, plan for her transportation, and finalize the required rider. With this last task complete, the planning process was over.

On the day of the party, James and I arrived a few hours early to do a walk-through with the hotel's event manager. We climbed the staircase to the ballroom and were blown away by the magnificent floral arrangement at the top of the stairs. But when we turned to face the ballroom, we were not prepared for how beautifully decorated the room was, with numerous floral arrangements mixed in with enormous candelabras. I could not recall ever seeing anything of this magnitude at any other event we had attended. We continued on to the reception area, which included four large photos of James hanging in the niches around the room, a beautiful ice carving of a Rolls Royce filled with shrimp, two bar stations, numerous seating areas, and more amazing floral arrangements throughout the room. The event manager said she had never seen these rooms so beautifully decorated and had taken numerous photos for her files, which confirmed to us that our goal of creating a memorable evening had been accomplished.

The hotel provided a suite for us to use prior to the guests' arrival. There were a variety of party appetizers prepared for us to sample. They knew that James would most likely not get to enjoy any of the food during the reception because he would be focused on welcoming friends as they arrived. We asked the family members to arrive an hour early so we could take photos of different family groups as well as one photo of the entire group. As guests began to arrive, they were shown to an area in the lobby that was beautifully decorated for a photo op and were provided with cards for their dinner-table assignment. As they ascended the staircase, they walked past numerous students from the Armstrong Community Music School playing violins. Once inside the reception area, guests were entertained by more students, who took turns playing the piano set up on a small stage.

After about an hour and a half, the guests were directed into the ballroom to be seated for dinner. I briefly spoke to welcome everyone and to introduce a friend of ours who would perform one of James' favorite songs while everyone was getting settled. To continue providing our guests with entertainment throughout the evening, we had a quartet perform classical music during dinner. James and I had a large table in the center of the room for a few close friends and family, and the other tables were scattered around the ballroom. At one point, I left the table and meandered throughout the room, stopping at various tables, making sure everything was going smoothly. Before dessert was served, James was seated on a throne on the stage, and his son Brad went up to say a few words about his dad, which was followed by performers from

ZACH Theatre singing a few of James' favorite songs. I chose the last song, which was Katy Perry's "Firework," and at the end of the song, the ballroom exploded into a multi-colored confetti storm. James was presented with a large birthday cake as members of Asleep at the Wheel, led by Ray Benson, sang "Happy Birthday."

Individual desserts were brought out to the guests, who were then invited to join us in the adjoining reception room, which had been transformed into a cabaret setting with a large dance floor. Asleep at the Wheel provided us with music to dance away the rest of this extraordinary evening.

Apparently, the party was a success as the following week, this article appeared in the local newspaper:

For a Mega-Benefactor, an Epic Party

It started with a card. It ended with a dance. And, in between, an epic birthday party.

Mega-benefactor James Armstrong turned 80 this week. His partner, Larry Connelly, started planning the salute to his eight decades five years ago. You could see the results last week at the Driskill Hotel.

Start with the David Kurio flower arrangements. Truckloads of orchids, roses, peonies, tulips in variations on fuchsia, peach, melon, and chartreuse. These volcanoes of floral glory competed with chandeliers towering over crimson tablecloths.

Move on to party planner Victoria Hentrich's stagecraft: Giant photos of Armstrong hanging in the ballroom, stuffed peacocks perched on banks of more flowers, a long feasting table for family members, and round banquet tables for other guests. Then there was the crowd. Particularly well-represented were backers of Zach Theatre, Austin Lyric Opera, Austin Symphony

Orchestra, Austin Cabaret Theatre, Ballet Austin, and various health and social charities.

Mela Sarajane Daily, Jill Blackwood, Jamie Goodwin, and Kelli Shultz performed American standards and a dance anthem. (Armstrong's tastes are catholic—he made Connelly take him to see Lady Gaga.). Son Brad Armstrong tried his hand at stand-up comedy during a fond salute to his father. Then Ray Benson and Asleep at the Wheel got folks onto their feet—those who didn't retired to the quieter lounge or coffee room.

What about the man? He's given away millions. Yet no more shy, thoughtful, and unpretentious benefactor could you meet.

He's clearly adored. While we all dined and danced on our host's dime, he asked that gifts be made to the Armstrong Community Music School, which recently separated from Austin Lyric Opera. What a guy!

Reprinted with permission
Austin American-Statesman
Thursday, May 17, 2012
Michael Barnes, p. D8

But the celebrating was not over yet, as we had one more party at El Greco. We invited about forty family members, along with friends who had come from out of town, to our home for dinner and surprise entertainment. I hadn't told anyone, including James, that Marilyn Maye would be performing a concert in our home. To keep it a surprise, I had to find a way to get James out of the house so she could arrive with her team to go through a rehearsal. I asked a couple of James' closest friends to take him out for lunch for a couple of hours, but he needed to be back home by 2:30 at the latest. I wanted him to take a nap when he returned, and I would sneak Marilyn into the house. She would have about an hour and a half to rehearse before she and her group would need to disappear downstairs until it was time to perform. The event planners brought in a company to transform the living room into an NYC cabaret and set up the guest rooms with refreshments and anything else Marilyn's people requested. Our florist brought in some of the flowers from the night before to make the room look stunning. He later sent me a list of the organizations where he sent the remaining flowers, which was a pleasant surprise for us and apparently much appreciated by the recipients.

A couple of friends came over around 5:00 p.m. to keep James company upstairs in his bedroom and to help him get ready for the party. Just before the guests started arriving, I went up to get them; no one knew yet what exactly was going on. We had a large luxury van bring the out-of-town guests from the hotel, so they all arrived together, and a few others arrived in their own vehicles. After about an hour of socializing, the guests were directed to find seats in the living room, and I began saying a few words of welcome and introducing the entertainment for the evening. In my speech, I mentioned that James was well known for often saying this phrase, "You can never have the same good time twice." I said I had always found this to be a challenge, and tonight was my attempt to prove this phrase wrong. I talked about James' fiftieth birthday party and how much he loved the woman who performed that evening. I said we had found her again performing in NYC, but that tonight she was going to perform just for us. Before I could say her name, James got the biggest smile on his face. He looked around and blurted out, "Where is she? Where is she?" I just continued with my introduction and said, "I would like to introduce you to the marvelous Marilyn Maye!" Her trio came in from the hallway, followed by Marilyn herself, to a large round of applause. I couldn't believe I had pulled this off. I enjoyed seeing surprised expressions from a few guests who were from NYC and had only seen her in cabaret shows and a few others who were actually at the fiftieth birthday party and couldn't believe she was now here.

Marilyn went on to perform for about an hour and a half, including rewriting the lyrics of a popular song specifically for James and me. She interacted with James throughout the concert and was delighted that we had two framed photos of them from his fiftieth on our table. After the concert, Marilyn went down to change, and we began directing guests to go to the kitchen, where we had a buffet dinner prepared for them. A little later, Marilyn joined us at our table. A waiter brought her a drink and said he would prepare a plate for her. James was having a wonderful time and could not stop smiling. He and Marilyn continued visiting for a couple of hours before she said she needed to leave. Before she left, we took a lovely new photo of the two of them that we placed at the end of the keepsake photo album from the weekend.

We talked about the party for many weeks and months to come. One thing James liked to point out was that he was so happy to have had the party because there was a small but growing list of people who would not be with us much longer, and we were happy to have created a wonderful event for them.

After a few months had passed, there were some health issues and safety concerns with James' ex-wife, and the kids determined she needed more assistance in her home. They spent the next couple of months developing a plan that would meet her needs. This opened up a discussion about James needing someone to assist him during the day. The owner of the administrator company James used to help organize his estate, Patti, found a man to come in each weekday. James resisted at first but agreed as long as he could still have his evenings and weekends free from in-home care. As it turned out, though, James didn't feel comfortable with this man, and after a while, he determined he did not want him coming to the house. We received a little blowback from the administrators and James' two older children, Brad and Liz, but James was determined to have him go. Patti said she would look for someone else for James, and she hired this man to assist her own husband. After a few weeks, she fired him as well because of his unpleasant personality and negative attitude, which reinforced James' decision to let him go.

Another caregiver was hired by the administrators, and it would turn out James would have issues with him as well. He didn't say much, didn't have much initiative, and would frequently sit on the sofa next to James' chair and fall asleep. James felt uncomfortable when this man would take him to appointments, fearing that he might have sleep apnea and fall asleep when driving. After a few weeks, James asked him not to return to the house. James felt that if he was going to have in-home care, it would need to be someone who was better trained and more professional, and someone James would feel comfortable having in our home.

I don't remember how they were found, but we met with a group called Nurse Case Management, who provided in-home caregivers as needed and would also be available to consult on James' health needs. Though we were getting some family pressure to have care 24/7, James would only agree to daytime care during the week; he still wanted us to have some privacy at night and on the weekends. The first couple of caregivers they sent us didn't work out for a variety of reasons, but after about a month, one of their longtime employees, Richard, became available, and James seemed comfortable with him helping us out.

After some time passed with in-home daytime assistance, James began thinking El Greco was no longer meeting his needs. The guest bathroom that he frequently used was small and difficult to access now that he needed someone to go in with him. He also could no longer go down to the pool level, and his master bathroom was becoming more difficult to navigate, with the carpeted flooring and the height of the step into the shower.

He heard about an assisted living facility that had private homes, apartments, and a health care center, so we made an appointment for a tour to see if it was something he would enjoy. We first looked at a few of the homes because they provided more privacy and independence, and we liked the layout. We then looked at the apartments and community areas and thought it was all well planned. When we met with the manager at the end of our tour, she said she could recommend a downsize expert they frequently used who could help us determine how much of our furniture we could fit into one of the units.

About a week later, the expert came to our home to make suggestions about what we could keep and what would need to be sold. She seemed very professional and made a lot of good suggestions. But after she left, James told me we were not going to sell anything, especially any of his large art collection. He said he wanted to live out the rest of his life in a home more suitable to his needs like his mother had done, and where he could keep everything. We made an appointment with our realtor, and James shared his idea to find a new home. What he was looking for was a newer home on one level with the master suite on the main floor. He wanted a three-car garage, a library, and lots of wall space for the art. The realtor said he felt he knew what we were looking for and said he hoped to have a few homes to look at in the next couple of weeks.

We went to look at the first home he found, which was brand new and had everything on James' wish list. The only problem was the location; it was far from the city and James' doctors, hospitals, many friends, and favorite restaurants. We asked our realtor to limit the search to the west side of town and less than five miles from our current location. He said it would definitely be a challenge and seriously limit our options, but he would try to find something. We looked at a few more homes in our area, but we always found something wrong with the houses. One house that was only three blocks from our current location, on Scenic, checked off a lot of our wants, but it was an older home that would require an extensive renovation. We were a little reluctant but agreed to look at it.

We toured the home and liked the sizes of the rooms; the layout would work well, including plenty of wall space for the art collection. The main issue was that it was highly decorated with ornate trim, and all of the wood on the walls made the rooms very dark. We were looking for a more contemporary style with clean lines that would place the focus on the art. We told our realtor we would consider this house but still wanted to check out more options.

After a few weeks had passed, our realtor let us know there were no other options at this time, so we decided to take our decorator to the home down the street to discuss what it would take to renovate it. She brought her construction manager with her, whom she was recommending for the job, so he could see what we wanted to do. We spent a long time at the house reviewing various design options, which gave us a lot to think about. When we left, we told our realtor we would think about it over the weekend and get back to him when we'd made our decision. After many conversations, we created the following pros-and-cons list for our current home on El Greco compared to this new house on Scenic:

El Greco

Pros	Cons
None	Too large/too much responsibility
	Multi-level
	High maintenance costs (old house)
	High utility costs
	Inaccessible pool

Scenic

Pros	Cons
Accessibility (single level)	None (after the renovation)
Lower utilities cost	
Lower maintenance costs	
Better lighting and wall space for art	
More room for desired belongings	

One thing that came from this exercise was James' growing concern about having enough money to live out the rest of his life. Though we knew the sale of El Greco would easily cover the cost of renovating Scenic, this wouldn't happen yet, as James didn't want to put it on the market until after we'd moved out. We talked about how before they restructured the estate plan, James didn't have this concern about his finances. Maybe changes could be made that would make him feel more financially comfortable; we appended this section to the bottom of our pros and cons list:

Bottom Line

At this point in his life, James should not be the one who is worried about his finances. We possibly need to look at restructuring the estate plan, so James has a source of income or access to new funds. Looking at the partnership's income source and Animal Pancakes' debt to James would be a starting point.

This list helped us determine James' final decision—to make an offer on the Scenic home and begin the renovation planning process. After a little negotiating, our offer was accepted, and we were pleased to be a step closer to achieving James' goal of creating a home where he could live out the rest of his life safely with all his belongings. However, the bottom line section seemed to be ignored, and nothing was done to make James feel more confident about his finances.

We spent the next month in multiple planning meetings with the contractor, who came to us highly recommended and had excellent references. We hadn't been involved in renovating a home before and relied on our decorator for guidance. In the end, we had a final plan that included everything on James' list of needs but with a sizable budget and a two-year timeline for completion. We were very satisfied and wanted to sign the contract to get the process started, but Patti felt the contract needed to be reviewed by a lawyer, and of course, at James' expense. This delayed us a few weeks because the lawyer, whom we didn't know, and Patti made numerous revisions and suggestions for changing the contract. We would review these changes with the contractor, many of which we did not agree with, but in the end, we did sign the contract, which ended up being almost identical to the original one presented to us. Fortunately for us, the contractor was not discouraged by this distraction, and we ended up having a great working relationship.

The next step was to hire an architect, which again was something we had never done before. We didn't know where to begin, and our decorator advised us on the selection process. She recommended one she had worked with many times. When we met with him, we were quite surprised by how young he was, but his resumé showed that he had worked with one of the top firms in the city for many years and had now started his own business. We decided to hire him. He worked with the contractor and us to review our plan, which he took back to his office to create design drawings for us. We met again a few weeks later, and he presented us with various indoor and outdoor elevations of the home. What impressed us was how he was able to use his computer to show us multiple views of the house from various perspectives. He also provided us with full-color photos of his designs for us to review at our convenience and help us determine any possible changes we might want to make. James really enjoyed these meetings and looking at the design drawings because it reminded him that as a young man, he enjoyed drawing perspectives of homes as a favorite hobby.

During this time, we realized how our weekly schedule was becoming more complicated. Along with numerous doctor visits and physical therapy appointments, we now had a few caregivers working with us, weekly meetings planning the renovation of the Scenic house, and we also needed to make repairs to the El Greco house for the eventual move and putting it on the market. A friend recommended we consider hiring a home manager to help keep us organized and to take on coordinating some of these duties, especially work projects at El Greco, the renovation at Scenic, and interviewing prospective caregivers when needed. This was a new idea for us, and we weren't sure how to find someone for this position. It turned out to be a lot easier than we could have hoped for. At a favorite restaurant for dinner one night, I was surprised to see someone I knew who lived in NYC. After he sat down, I went over to his table to say hello. He introduced me to the two young men he was visiting, who had recently moved to Austin. We spoke for a few minutes, and I updated him on our plans to move and mentioned that we were now looking for a home manager to help us out. One of his friends, Nick, said he was surprised by what I just said because he had just started working for a business that provided home managers and other services for private homeowners. This was excellent news, and we agreed to get in touch so he could visit with James and me to tell us more about the company and would he be able to help us. When James and I were ready to leave the restaurant, we stopped by my friend's table to introduce James and confirm that we were interested in meeting about the home manager position.

About a week later, we met with Nick at El Greco and showed him around the property talking about what projects we needed to do over the next couple of years. We also showed him plans of the Scenic home and the construction schedule. He told us about the company he worked for and about the variety of services they could provide based on our needs and said that he personally would be the one to oversee our household. Over our two-hour meeting, Nick answered our questions and concerns, and we said we would get back to him with our decision. James and I spent the next few days talking about what a home manager could do for us and possibly move forward with hiring Nick. Since there was no long-term commitment, we couldn't determine a downside and decided to give it a try. As it turned out, we were very happy with this decision. We were freed up from our many scheduling conflicts because Nick could make himself available for some appointments when we needed to be somewhere else. Our household would continue to expand, but hiring Nick would prove to be the best decision we could have made.

Chapter 8

IT HITS THE FAN

On January 12, 2015, I received an e-mail from Brad. I noticed it was also copied to Liz and Patti. It was sent out of the blue, not related to any specific incident, and truly caught me off guard. In it, he made a number of harsh accusations about me that just didn't make any sense. In the end, he threatened to not sign the contract for the Scenic renovations unless things improved. I found this interesting because I don't think James needed Brad's permission since the Scenic project was James' decision and his money being used. I also wondered how Brad would explain this decision to his dad and what James' reaction would be.

I wasn't sure how to respond to this e-mail as I was upset at the unfounded accusations he was making but didn't want to start an argument, so I decided to take the high road to see if I could get some specific details from him or to at least better understand his motives. So I asked him for more details or specific examples about what he had written.

I was hopeful my e-mail response would appease Brad or at least shift him from an attack mode to something more productive to try and resolve his issues. But I was sorely mistaken. The next day he responded with misperceptions of what he thought was going on at El Greco. He asserted that James had repeatedly told Brad and others that he didn't want to move. I knew it could be difficult to be in Colorado and not know day-to-day details about El Greco happenings, but I didn't know what sources Brad was using to make these statements, and I found it all very confusing. The statements about James being confused or stressed out about the move and renovation were nonsense. James looked forward to our weekly construction update meetings, selecting tile, paint colors, carpeting, and fixtures, and he frequently requested visiting the Scenic home to check on the progress of the renovation. Not once did I hear him say he didn't want to move or that he had any regrets about his decision to move to Scenic. The other thing that bothered me was that Brad did not seem to know his father very well because when it comes to spending money, James didn't listen to anyone else; ultimately, though he would discuss things, he made his financial decisions himself. Over all the years we spent together, I did not ask or persuade James to spend money on any major expenses, including cars, trips, or homes.

Brad's response did not help me determine what he was trying to accomplish or what I needed to do next. Over the next month, I shared this e-mail with various people I had regular contact with to get some direction, but they were equally confused. Their responses to Brad's e-mail usually fell into one of three categories: they questioned his intellect and education level, his mental stability, or his emotional stability. One person was specific when he said he normally questioned people who overuse absolutes in their writing. My therapist said this e-mail was evidence of someone who considered himself entitled and who was self-centered. His advice to me was to realize that I could not change other people's behavior, but I could protect myself by creating barriers. He then helped me develop these barriers, and I immediately put them into place.

I shared this e-mail during a meeting with Nick and Debbie (our consultant with Nurse Case Management) to get ideas about what to do next. Debbie said she had seen things like this before with families she'd worked with and suggested that I consult a lawyer to create ways to protect myself in case things got worse. This suggestion startled me a bit, but I decided to take her advice and called a lawyer I knew well. Even though this situation did not fall into her area of expertise, she was the only one I trusted. After going down the list she provided, I was able to select a lawyer who worked with families and said he thought he could help. After we had our first meeting, he asked me to return in a couple of weeks, when he would have a plan of action to share with me.

On January 14, 2015, I sent the following e-mail to James' children:

The meeting today with Debbie from Nurse Case Management went very well. Nick is in Dallas and Patti was home with the flu so it was your dad, Richard and me at the meeting. Highlights include:

- searching for an evening person to come in every night
- adding weekend assistance
- purchasing a walker and transport wheelchair to have on hand when needed
- installing a bed handle on your dad's bed to assist with getting up
- checking in to some physical therapy during the week
- a possible back-up generator for the elevator
- we all agreed Richard and Nick were great additions to the household

Until more staff are in place, Richard is going to begin coming in on Saturdays and Sundays for the morning routine and I will continue going up at night to assist with the bedtime routine.

Debbie is going to write up a more detailed summary after she checks on a few things and I'll make sure you get a copy when we receive it. Let me know if you have questions.

Larry

Liz responded to this e-mail the same day: "Thanks Larry. These seem like great assessments & decisions."

Brad's response was a little less supportive. He basically said to stop talking to his dad about things Brad had been saying to me because it caused James "great, ongoing worry." One example he gave was that James had called Jennifer at the estate administrator's office distressed, totally confused, and stressed out. But then Brad said that things appeared to be "much more pleasant and productive around the house the last couple of days." I'm not sure what he was referring to since it had only been two days since his first e-mail attack, and nothing had been changed at the house. Good grief! What an ass. Don't talk to his dad about all this. Really?

It truly bothered me when Brad painted a portrait of his dad not having the ability to process information or mentioned dementia. It's almost like he wanted James to be unable to function. I specifically asked his doctors if James had dementia, and they all said no. James was going out to dinner many nights a week, hosting dinner parties, and attending many social functions each month. He was very interactive with people and able to carry on conversations without any issues. I just didn't understand what Brad was trying to accomplish by these unsubstantiated attacks, and I needed to come up with another response. The other thing that bothered me about this e-mail was that if James had called Jennifer in distress, why hadn't Richard or Jennifer said something to me about it? Richard had to have been present and surely would have alerted me about it. Since Richard had said nothing, I had to believe that what Brad described had not happened.

Since Brad was still on the attack, and I needed another plan of action, I enlisted Nick's assistance. We decided he could take more of a Swiss role and become the neutralizer to defuse the situation, and we developed a new communication system I had used in my school when I was the principal. The purpose was to get everything out in the open, provide an accurate picture of James' condition, and hopefully protect me from any more personal attacks. Nick sent out this e-mail the following week and included all the actors involved with our household, including all three of James' kids, James' estate administrators (Patti and Jennifer), and Debbie and the caregivers from Nurse Case Management:

Hello—

I hope you are having a lovely start to the New Year!

Today we are implementing a new tool of communication to keep everyone accurately informed on the happenings and progress at the Armstrong/Connelly household.

Larry made the suggestion for us to open and deepen the communication between all parties. My suggestion was to send out a weekly newsletter. Please feel free to write a letter to the editor by pressing REPLY ALL.

Welcome to the very first, highly anticipated, hot off the presses.....

"El Greco Gazette"
January 12–January 23
Mr. Armstrong had the following appointments.

- Chiropractor for his bi-weekly appointment to address his neuropathy.
- Dermatologist for his quarterly checkup.
- Dentist to replace a crown.
- Pilates for his weekly agility training.
- Massage for weekly muscle relaxation.

January 14th:

Debbie Pearson from Nurses Case management came to perform a re-assessment of the home health care system that is currently in place. She was incredibly helpful and offered praise for the current system and encouraged us to focus our energies in certain areas. I have attached her re-assessment for your reference. I cannot stress enough how lucky we are to be working with Debbie Pearson and her team at Nurses Case Management. Their vast professionalism and capability matched with their personal care and open hearts instill such comfort in what could be a very uncomfortable time.

January 15th:

Richard began administering Mr. Armstrong's Parkinson's related medications to him upstairs. This is about half an hour earlier in the morning routine than it has been. This was recommended by Nurses Case Management.

We had a walk through at the Scenic home to discuss the status of the demolition. Mr. Armstrong, Larry, Richard and myself were all present. It was a very productive meeting. We were able to ask questions of the contractor and have things explained. Mr. Armstrong was very excited about the visit and articulated his enthusiasm about the project to the contractor and to us. This meeting will become part of our weekly schedule. It will enable us to stay on top of the project's progression and include all parties in decision-making and problem solving.

January 16th:

We had our first full session with our professional organizer Susan Nolley. She came highly recommended by Donna Stockton Hicks. We had met with Susan before the holidays to discuss the specific needs of the household and set some organizational/purging goals. We could not have asked for a better first session. Mr. Armstrong really responded to her energy. They spent about two hours going through Mr. Armstrong's closet. They organized, they purged, they donated, and they told stories. It is an excellent exercise for Mr. Armstrong to go through his items and be able to articulate the stories behind them. Susan will be a bi-weekly appointment at the Armstrong/Connelly residence. We believe this service will benefit the overall health and flow of the entire household. Susan will be working with Mr. Armstrong to organize his personal areas to avoid confusion and clutter.

January 17th and January 18th:

This is the first weekend that Richard started offering his services in the mornings. It was a seamless transition. Richard arrived at 10:00 a.m. and was able to assist Mr. Armstrong in the shower and with getting dressed. We have eliminated all opportunities for Mr. Armstrong to slip in the shower by providing 7 day-a-week care for the morning routine. This weekend assistance will continue indefinitely.

January 20:

Larry purchased a four-wheeled walker to assist Mr. Armstrong in times when he might need it. Mr. Armstrong and Larry had their meeting with Patti and Jennifer at the home. It was an incredibly positive and communicative meeting. I began the meeting by giving an update on the Scenic household and offered Patti and Jennifer a snap shot of where we are in terms of at-home health care.

January 21:

Richard introduced the product called "Thick It" to Mr. Armstrong's drinking water. This was a suggestion from Nurses Case Management to assist in Mr. Armstrong's coughing that occurs sometimes when he is taking medications.

January 22:

We had our weekly meeting with the contractor at Scenic. The interior demolition process is going smoothly and enabling the contractor to see the potential of the home. We were introduced to a prospective architect during this meeting. We were able to stress the importance of implementing safety measures throughout the design of the home for Mr. Armstrong's long-term health, comfort and safety. He will begin creating some design drawings for approval. Mr. Armstrong had a few recommendations and was able to walk through the house, make decisions and articulate them to the contractor. He used his four-wheeled walker during this walk through. He was confident and enjoyed using it. When we got back to El Greco Mr. Armstrong said "I have a proclamation...I am pleased with the work that is being done at Scenic." It made me happy to hear this.

January 23:

We have another full session scheduled with Susan Nolley. She will continue her organization/purging work with Mr. Armstrong.

Weekly Observations and Discussions:

There is a lot of new energy and tools for wellbeing/safety being introduced to the household. I am pleased with the spirit of acceptance from everyone.

We have to be very careful not to overwhelm Mr. Armstrong in the process of assistance. He is always willing to let me know when he has had enough and for that I am appreciative. He has done just that.

Mr. Armstrong has stated that he is not willing to have an overnight caretaker at this time. He does not feel comfortable with having someone down the hall from him in the night-time hours. We spoke about this as a group. We had an open conversation about the benefits of nighttime care. Mr. Armstrong is firm in his decision that this is not something he wants or will accept at this point.

Mr. Armstrong has also stated that he is not willing to have a physical therapist come to the house for weekly visits. He feels comfortable with his Pilates and is not willing to introduce a physical therapist at this point. He exercises daily with Richard and attends Pilates weekly. We had an open conversation where we spoke about the benefits of physical therapy and its effects on long-term mobility. He is firm in his decision that this is not something he wants or will accept at this point.

Debbie Pearson is on vacation for the next week. I will be speaking with her when she returns to discuss Mr. Armstrong's desires and how we can all work together to make sure we are not implementing too much at once and creating unnecessary anxiety for Mr. Armstrong.

Communication and teamwork are at an all time high on El Greco Cove. Richard continues to provide Mr. Armstrong with exceptional care Monday through Friday from 8:45 a.m. to 4:45 p.m. and Saturday/Sunday care from 10:00 a.m. to 11:00 a.m. Larry is taking the lead on scheduling the week's appointments and overseeing the overall flow of the household. I assist when needed. I will continue my journalistic ambition every Friday with the "El Greco Gazette." Please feel free to use this weekly periodical as a catalyst for productive conversations based off the topics provided.

In Other News:

Lucky continues to chase the ball and behave like a very adorable dog. We are thrilled to watch him as he continues to obsess over ice and treats.

Have a wonderful weekend!

Best,
Nick Mayo

Brad's response on January 25, 2015, was:

Dear All,

I think the Gazette is a great idea and tool to keep us all simultaneously abreast of El Greco happenings. Thanks to Larry and Nick for getting it started.

Basically, I have little to say except: keep it up—earlier administration of meds on an empty stomach (yes, we can have no bananas!); further safeguards; exercise and activity to foster dad's mobility, strength, balance, etc.

I am pleased that Dad has re-asserted his excitement and commitment to moving ahead with the Scenic remodel. I worry that the project is very stressful for all involved and thinks it's very important that it's a net-positive for Dad, given his adverse reaction to stress of any nature.

Fantastic on the organizing—it sounds like Susan has an extraordinary set of skills simply being an organizer. And that Dad gets to recall and tell stories related to all the encountered objects—what a bonus!

About the overnight caretaker. It is important that Dad get this help as expeditiously as possible. However, as Nick points out, there is a lot of change happening quite suddenly and it's good to "make sure we are not implementing too much at once and creating unnecessary anxiety" for Dad. Perhaps we could set a goal to introduce night help within a month rather than, say, ASAP? Perhaps some modification could be proposed to Dad—for instance, that the caregiver stay on the main floor, constantly monitoring, and be available very quickly, without Dad being made to feel so crowded and vulnerable? And it might help to remind Dad that the nighttime caregiver would be there 10:00 until Richard's arrival—virtually invisible unless needed. Another idea might be to have the new caregiver shadow Richard for several days in his routine with Dad, to break the ice.

PT would be great, but Dad is currently getting a vastly improved range of options for movement and exercise. Again, perhaps there is a way to re-frame the issue of a "physical therapist," so it's less invasive for Dad?

Thanks everybody for all the great progress.

yours,
Brad

WOW! What a change in tone now that we had an audience reading everything sent out, especially considering that Brad's initial attack e-mail had only been a few weeks prior. Everyone now had to "reply all" versus sending individual responses, so everyone in the loop knew what was being said. When people didn't "reply all," Nick corrected them and made them do it over. The gazette was working as a successful system that would keep Brad off my back. As the weeks went by, there were no more attack e-mails and I hoped it would stay that way.

The gazette on the week of February 16–22, 2015, contained the following concerns that James had been expressing:

Weekly Observations and Discussions:

It has been a very full week at the Armstrong/Connelly household. There has been some resistance that has occurred over the weekend. Mr. Armstrong has stated that he feels like everyone is crowding around him and telling him what to do. He is exercising his power and using his voice to be very declarative about what he wants and doesn't want.

When I arrived this morning 2-23-15 I was told by Mr. Armstrong that he does not want a back up caregiver. He is unwilling to move forward with this step. We all tried to convince him that this was an important and necessary step in his long-term care. He spoke about his mother and the care that she received. He wants to stay in his home and continue the support he has right now. He is asking for space. Larry mentioned to Mr. Armstrong that the reason that Mr. Armstrong's mother was able to stay in her home until the age of 95 was because she had a strong staff and support system. Mr. Armstrong did not want to hear this. He said he was pleased with the level of care he was receiving now. He is pleased with Richard and very thankful for his assistance. At the end of a long conversation Mr. Armstrong said "Ok, I will think about it...Just to make you happy."

We have a meeting scheduled with Debbie Pearson in two weeks. We will lean on her to assist in this challenge. This is very tricky. This backup person is necessary.

In Other News:

It's going to be a very cold week. We plan on spending a lot of time by the fire and exercising.

Best,
Nick

Brad responded on February 24 with the following:

I think Liz's last suggestion is a good one.

I have heard this kind of thing from lots of people I've talked to about caring for older people—resistance to change, to too much care, to feeling out of control. So I think it's typical and understandable, which still doesn't make it an insignificant problem, because Dad needs adequate care and Larry and Richard need relief from their caretaker roles.

It is our job to see that Dad is taken care of sufficiently, and his job to occasionally resist. If he falls and is injured, all of this will be moot. So I feel like the team might have to push back harder (in as kind and gentle a fashion as is possible—again, perhaps following Liz's suggestion) than we feel comfortable doing in order to keep Dad safe and the care system humming.

I will say once again how much I appreciate this gazette forum, which helps us all stay headed in the same direction.

B.

This is the e-mail from Liz that Brad was referencing:

I am so relieved & thrilled that dad has his voice heard. It is our responsibility as his "team" to interpret what is really going on.

You are all doing a great job. It is also HUGE that Richard is supported. He is first line of care. (And a great hugger)

The suggestion from Liz that Brad thought was a good one:

> I was also wondering if the conversation came from the direction of how much the routine helps Larry and supports Larry that it might put a different value to it for dad? (Just a thought.)

Now all of a sudden they were concerned with my welfare? That is rich! But I was going to take what I could get and hoped this new system of communication would keep everyone happy and content.

Using our gazette format for the first time, Debbie sent the following report to the group:

> Subject: Armstrong meeting 3-4-15
>
> Hello all. Just wanted to forward my visit notes from today. Please let me know if you have any questions or concerns.
>
> Met with Larry first to see if he could help me problem solve with how to convince Mr. Armstrong to allow a 2nd caregiver in so that we could have a back-up + so that Richard could have a day off a week. Larry said that it seems Mr. Armstrong is simply having too much done for him by others and he thinks that this may be a contributor to why we saw the "push back" with the 2nd person. EVERYONE is fully supportive of bringing in another person but Mr. Armstrong is in the current mindset of proving his abilities, not wanting more help. This is both understandable and a stance that will go a long way in helping him function at his optimal level. It is good for him but bad for our planning to avert a disaster. Larry's insight was helpful for me to better understand the issue before meeting with Mr. Armstrong.

I then met with Mr. Armstrong who was as pleasant as ever but I could tell it was a day where he was having more of a struggle with complex thoughts. In talking about the 2nd caregiver we brought in to meet him (Emanuel), there seemed to be some confusion that this represented more than one person working with him at a time or else expanding the caregiver hours. I assured him that the hours would be the same as the current schedule and that there would only be one caregiver at a time after the new one was fully trained. Larry pointed out that training is needed to assure continuity of care; very true. Mr. Armstrong then said he could not understand Emanuel who does have an accent. This is an issue that is common in our industry because of the number of non-Caucasian workers in this industry. It was obvious to me that Mr. Armstrong was willing to be cooperative but was having trouble following the complex discussion of needing a back-up for potential staffing problems and the training time needed. As a result, I narrowed the discussion to a "Tuesday worker" and he agreed for me to continue the search for a Tuesday worker—male, easy to understand, not pushy. I assured him this person does exist but may take me some time to identify. He authorized me to continue the search with more specific qualifications. Going forward, I think if we limit the discussion to the "Tuesday worker" then it will become more easily understood.

Then I met with Richard who said he is fine continuing 6 days a week until we find that perfect person. Richard agreed to notify me if he believes he is becoming worn down from the current schedule. The household is a pleasant team of people who all care about Mr. Armstrong's well being so it is a very positive job for Richard that is not causing him stress. He assured me NCM can take the time to get the right person. I believe I will need to do some personal networking but eventually will find a fit.

These notes will be emailed to everyone in the home today, the children, and Personal Administrators, & Candy Swain.

Thanks,
Debbie

I was really happy to have Debbie send out these reports because they were so well written and were wonderful examples of how to constructively communicate. In this report, I especially liked the following statement:

> The household is a pleasant team of people who all care about Mr. Armstrong's well being so it is a very positive job for Richard that is not causing him stress.

This is yet another example that contradicted Brad's attacks and demonstrated how far he distorted reality to suit his needs. I was unable to determine where all of that anger came from; it didn't surface again. I still wondered from time to time about the cause and if it would surface again.

The next month went by without incident. The caregiver situation was going well, we were enjoying having Nick on board, and he was working out well. And James was in good spirits and heavily involved in the renovation project. I sent out the following notes to the group on May 21 about James' medical planning meeting, including discussing the Medical Power of Attorney (MPOA):

> Here are the notes from yesterday's meeting with Debbie from Nurse Case Management. We covered quite a bit but are having another meeting next week to finish off the list of things for James to make decisions about his future care.
>
> I thought everything went well and look forward to the next meeting.
>
> Larry

Begin forwarded message:

From: Debbie

Here are my notes from today's meeting in the home. Please let me know if you have any questions or we need to talk. It's nice to be making progress.

Meeting with Larry (+ Nick present) first to discuss some care related topics that I would like to "test the waters" before discussing with Mr. Armstrong. It is time for us to look at future medical planning while Mr. A can clearly articulate his wishes for care as he ages. Mr. A still clearly has capacity to both make decisions and articulate his wishes. Two of the first items to be addressed are code status (DNR?) and feeding tube. These items were discussed with Larry:

We discussed the EMS form that must be completed in advance, signed, witnessed, and signed by the PCP. This is the only way EMS/Paramedics who come to the home have documentation to NOT do cardio-pulmonary-resuscitation. If this is not completed and available, they must do CPR. I explained that the EMS form is only for CPR in the home. It is not utilized in the hospital as each hospitalization stands on its own. A discussion with the treating doctor has to take place to determine CPR status based on the reason for the hospitalization.

The other item is in regard to a feeding tube. With the progression of Parkinson's, swallowing becomes more difficult. At some point, most patients can no longer take in enough food and fluids to meet their health needs. In these situations, a feeding tube can be placed directly into the stomach (small outpatient surgery) so that the tube can be utilized to maintain adequate nutrition and hydration. With a feeding tube, then eating and drinking can be simply for pleasure.

The third thing we talked about had to do with Medical POA. Larry is first with Brad 2nd, Liz 3rd, Tony 4th. There was an open discussion about how difficult it can be for the MPOA to be the decision maker as health status changes. This can be a highly emotional and difficult role. It is made easier by Mr. A's wishes for care to be clearly documented while he is mentally clear. One never wants to wait for an emergent change to make care wishes known. Mr. A's wishes are the guide for care and anyone who is in this role has an obligation to follow the wishes. However, a great collaborative and supportive group is essential to lessen the load. If there is to be any amendment to the MPOA document, it needs to be done while Mr. A has capacity.

The Medical Planning Worksheet was briefly presented as a working document for wishes. It is not possible to complete today but can likely be done in two meetings.

Adding a second caregiver must be done—based on best clinical experience and personality fit. We cannot wait any longer but need to get Nick to do initial meetings with the qualified candidates.

Larry believed the most important items could be openly discussed with Mr. A so we then went to that meeting. I was advised to stay on topic without too many examples to cause confusion. This is what was discussed/decided at this meeting:

Mr. A was willing to discuss advance medical planning so I could document wishes.

He was clear that he would not want CPR in the home. He signed the EMS form that I will get to his physician for signature. Once this is fully executed, I will make multiple copies and keep them easily accessible in the home.

He is okay with a feeding tube for supplemental feeds when/ if this becomes necessary. This is a simple procedure and the caregivers can be trained on the use and care.

Mr. A agreed to the Tuesday caregiver to be screened and placed. We will move forward with this. The hours will be 8:30 a.m.–2:30 p.m. Nick will screen the candidates. Richard will do the one-on-one training.

A meeting for next week was scheduled to complete the rest of the Medical Planning Worksheet.

One other thing came up at the meeting that I can only offer many apologies. I have been quite remiss in not including Tony in the medical planning talks. I know he has just had a huge loss to deal with and may be very emotionally drained. However, I will reach out to him by email and phone so he is included in "Team Armstrong." The stronger and more inclusive the planning team the better. This was my oversight and will not happen again.

Debbie

Another fine example of how well Debbie was able to communicate so clearly, even with difficult information. During our portion of the meeting, she went into great detail about how difficult it can be to make some medical decisions, especially given that James did not want to be resuscitated. She wanted to make sure I could follow James' wishes. And again, she found a quiet way to counter Brad's false assessment of James when she stated: "Mr. A still clearly has capacity to both make decisions and articulate his wishes."

I really appreciated these kinds of notes inserted into her reports because everyone in the group was reading them and was now getting an accurate description of James' health and mental status.

Things continued to go well over the next few months, but every once in a while we had a little hiccup. Nick sent out the following incident report on June 26, 2015:

Team Armstrong—

I hope you all are well and enjoying this summer season. It has been a lovely and wet summer in Austin, TX.

There was a minor incident that occurred on Wednesday night at El Greco Cove. I want to keep you all informed at all times of happenings in the home. I hesitated to even deem this newsworthy, but I would rather over share than under share. This event happened Wednesday night.

Mr. Armstrong woke up in the middle of the night to use the restroom. Larry was able to hear him on the monitor and headed upstairs to offer assistance. Mr. Armstrong used the restroom and Larry and Mr. Armstrong both went back to sleep. A few hours later Larry heard Mr. Armstrong stirring on the monitor again. He went upstairs and Mr. Armstrong had experienced difficulties getting out of the bed and was sitting on the floor by the bed. Larry assisted Mr. Armstrong to the restroom and slept in the chair by Mr. Armstrong's bed until he went back to sleep.

Mr. Armstrong spoke of this incident on Thursday morning. He said that he was not injured or scared. We asked him if there is any support or adjustments to his bed that he would like for us to make. He said no. We asked if he would like an additional bed handle and he said that he was comfortable with his current bed handle.

Richard asked Mr. Armstrong if he was hurt and he said no. He was able to examine him thoroughly during their morning routine and reported no physical cuts or bruises.

We have made adjustments to Mr. Armstrong's bed and mattress to avoid situations like this. Mr. Armstrong mentioned that his sheets are a bit slippery. We will provide another sheet option for him. We will continue to search for more tools and will lean on Debbie and Nurses Case Management for their professional guidance in regards to equipment that might assist with this. Mr. Armstrong and Larry have a meeting with Debbie and Candice next Tuesday. This will be discussed.

I share this in the spirit of communication and not for alarm. I feel like the more everyone is informed the better we can work as a team. Please let me know if you have any questions or concerns that you would like to discuss further.

Best,
Nick

Liz responded with this:

Nick, et all...

Thank you. APPRECIATE THIS...and yet my immediate thought & comment is that we all have been operating in an expectation of team communication all along. To only hear this on Friday, and to know that it was considered to be kept secret, causes me ponder & concern that we are still working on two different team tables.....you all at el Greco & the rest of us at the kids/appeasing table. I'm so glad no injury occurred, the monitors worked, new avenues of "fixin" what doesn't work are being sought & implemented....but I still feel we are not a team.

Let's put this on the list as well please.

This stuff isn't pretty, but it's reality.

This said, WHAT AN AMAZING DAY IN THE HISTORY OF THE UNITED STATES OF AMERICA! Happy Marriage Equality Ya'll.

love & hugs.
Liz

This was typical Liz. Somehow she could take a situation about someone else and turn it around so the focus was on her (pity party for one, please). We took the time and made an effort to keep the communication going with no effort on her part, but whenever possible, she found a way to turn something positive into a negative. Fortunately, Debbie saw a possible problem brewing and felt Nick needed more praise and appreciation for what he was doing and quickly sent out the following:

Nick, what a blessing you are!! I know how busy the Armstrong household can be and appreciate that you were able to take the time to sit down and put this amount of detail and follow-up steps into the team communication.

Liz, I received your response and have to tell you how very much I appreciate your comments. Open and honest communication is critical to us getting things right all the way around. The reality is that there are always two levels of communications with an extended team. The team that is "boots on the ground" takes care of whatever is happening real time. When something happens, 100% of the response, effort, and communication must be directed at the situation at hand. From what I heard, that is exactly what occurred. Having been there so much of my career in health care, I continue to be surprised how long a thoughtful response takes. This is especially true in situations like your dad's. Talks with Mr. Armstrong can take two to three days in order to reach the time when he is cognitively clear. It looks like Nick took the time to have a physical exam be done, talk with your dad about options, and get in touch with me to set up a meeting.

With family out of town, I have seen communication happen immediately with the event only and no follow up. Those do not go well as it appears there has been no action in response to the incident. If you could allow us some time to respond with the whole picture, I really think this will be more acceptable. We do have a very caring team with all clearly focused on your dad's best interest. If you can allow us time to get you the well put together type email that Nick sent, then this allows us to put all the focus where it needs to be in the immediate moment.

I am totally open to your thoughts as you are excellent at being open and honest regarding your thoughts. If you believe I am off base with regard to this team, please let me know.

Thanks,
Debbie

What a pro! We were so fortunate to have her play such an active role in supporting James and our ever-growing household. She had a clear understanding of how to respond to Liz when she went on a tangent and to get her back on track with a focus on James' well being.

That didn't last long, though. Liz sent the following on July 1, 2015:

Good Morning All,

Hope this finds you well. I am just departing Austin after having some nice time with Dad & Larry in between doing legal paperwork on Mom's estate.

I wanted to communicate one curious conversation Dad initiated last night at dinner that I found surprising. (Happy surprise) Larry was present as well and, although I can't speak for his reaction, I know the look of surprise was on his face.

Dad brought up, out of the blue, that he had decided to start looking for and hiring someone to be with him overnight. After recovering from my shock I said I was really happy about that idea. He responded that he wasn't particularly happy about it but he knew it was necessary.

Has anyone else heard Dad have a change of heart on the overnight idea? I think we're all still on board with this idea, right?

He also mentioned his understanding of how much he DOES NOT REMEMBER and that decisions he makes are quickly gone. He is often overwhelmed with too much information and too many questions. We talked about how nice it is to have a trusted team in place with people who understand what he wants for the most part. I encouraged him to trust that above all we know he wants to remain in a life style that he is accustomed to (he exclaimed "that's right"). I said "you want to be in your house surrounded by your art, your collected antiques, your loving partner, children & dog, your movies of old and long time friends." Again he said "that's right!"

Thanks again to everyone on this team that helps keep dad the strongest & safest & best he can be. We all know this is an ever changing palette. I consider you each an angel and blessing for my dad & our family.

Hugs to all
Liz

Oh brother, she just didn't get it. "I know the look of surprise was on his face" was pure cluelessness. How did she not understand that I was present for all meetings, discussions, and decision-making? Of course, I knew about the addition of an overnight caregiver. But I didn't need to respond to this and other inaccuracies in her e-mail because Nick stepped in with the following response:

Liz—

I am happy to hear that you had a good conversation with your father in regards to the care that he is receiving.

There are continued efforts at play to make certain that Mr. Armstrong's care is evolving with him. Under the guidance of Nurses Case Management we are encouraged to stay active within this process.

The goal is for Mr. Armstrong and Larry to continue the lifestyle that they are accustomed to by introducing the caregiving professionals necessary to insure Mr. Armstrong's safety within this lifestyle.

Richard continues to offer exceptional care. The care relationship that is developing between Richard and Mr. Armstrong is a gift to observe. You used the word angel in your email. Richard is an angel!

Justin Herrera has been introduced to the care team and everyone is eager for this care relationship to succeed.

The overnight caregiving position has always been a piece of the ongoing conversation that the care team has. Debbie and Candice came to the house for a meeting yesterday afternoon to continue this conversation.

Debbie reiterated that she believes that there is a need for a nighttime caregiver. She reported that in her experience she has witnessed many incidents that occur during the nighttime hours. In order to stay ahead of this issue she reintroduced her opinion that a nighttime caregiver should be implemented.

Mr. Armstrong has not liked the idea of having someone down the hall from him in the nighttime hours. Debbie, Candice and Larry encouraged Mr. Armstrong to give it a try. They stressed that it was an important piece of care that he deserves. At the end of the conversation Mr. Armstrong said that he would think about it. He has given us permission to begin interviewing candidates for this position.

There are many people working to ensure that Mr. Armstrong and Larry have every opportunity to succeed. The FAMILY team, the CARE team, the FINANCIAL team, the RENOVATION team are all pivotal in this couple's success. Doing our jobs and recommitting ourselves to the part we play within team ARMSTRONG is a goal I believe we all share.

Thank you for your continued support. As always, please feel free to "reply all" to receive the support of this group.

-Nick-

But Liz wasn't going to let it go and responded:

Thanks Nick,

I did not know that Debbie & Candace had had a meeting with Dad & Larry yesterday. That must have been the "possible" meeting at 4:15 mentioned on the gazette. It's good to know where his thought track came from.

Everyone is so valuable on this team and you did a great job at describing the various tangents of Dad's world. I'm so thrilled that Richard will get some much needed aid & support with the addition of Justin. It is more happy news that you confirm Dad's willingness to let the team start looking for a night time care giver. I will hope that brings an added reduction of stress and continued support for Larry.

It was nice to see you Monday. Sorry to miss Debbie & Candace yesterday and the meeting. My late afternoon was free and I could have joined you. Larry will recall I checked into the afternoon schedule to see if there were any visiting times possible after dad's rest & before dinner. Clearly another opportunity in this dance of working together missed. Let's keep working on it.

I look forward to what tomorrow brings.

Hugs to all, liz

This time Nick felt the need to call Liz directly to respond to her e-mail. Specifically, the statement about another missed opportunity to work together needed a response. Nick let her know she wasn't invited to the meeting because one of the other purposes of getting together was to discuss the latest round of e-mails from her and how best to address them to prevent any possible problems since for the most part, things had been going well, and we wanted to keep it that way. I believe she got the message because she began communicating in a more supportive and positive fashion.

Another thing that puzzled me about Liz and Brad requesting all of this information from us was that they could have set up meetings with NCM staff anytime they were visiting from Colorado. To my recollection, this only happened one time, and I wondered why they didn't do it more often. It would have been a wonderful opportunity for them to get answers to their questions, address any concerns, and have a better understanding of the planning process to meet James' needs and goals—all from a neutral party. This truly was the "missed opportunity."

We also had a couple of phone calls from Brad, who would go off on something he'd been told that was completely off base. In one call, he complained that we were having renovation meetings and making decisions behind James' back. When he called, we were heading out the door to a doctor's appointment. Nick took the call, and as we were leaving, I heard Nick say something like, "I don't know where you are getting your information, but what you are saying couldn't be further from the truth, and I think you might need to get some new sources." He told me later that he felt he'd addressed Brad's false charges and hoped it wouldn't happen again.

The only other call I can remember happened after we moved to Scenic, and Brad wanted me on the phone out of earshot from his dad—always a concerning request. He was asking about something his dad had said in a recent phone call about an upcoming meeting they were having. I said I didn't know what he was talking about since it was clear from the e-mail that was sent out, I was not invited to the meeting and didn't even know what it was about. He then went on about how often James brought up concerns about his finances and was there something I could do. I let him know he was talking to the wrong person, as it was Patti who would keep telling James how he was "debt-heavy" (the D-word), which was something James had never had issues with in the past before they restructured the estate plan. I also mentioned how she had stopped providing him with brief financial updates of his net worth, specifically, the monthly amounts of income that seemed to make James comfortable about his wealth. Brad told me I should speak to her about it, but I let him know that she didn't listen to me any more than he did, so it would be up to him to address this situation. I wasn't certain he was listening to anything I said, but sure enough, the next time he was in town for a family meeting, he said Patti brought up the "D" word, and he told her to stop using that word. I don't remember any more attack calls after that; I believe the "source" was finally put in her place.

The next day, we had an incident that helped us convince James he needed more support. Nick sent out the following on July 2, 2015:

Team—

I hope you are well and enjoying the beginning of this holiday weekend.

I am writing to keep you informed of any and all happenings in regards to Mr. Armstrong and his care.

After having a very productive meeting with Debbie and Candice about the need for overnight care, Mr. Armstrong and Larry navigated an incident that has made the necessity much more immediate.

In the early morning hours on Wednesday Mr. Armstrong had another incident.

Please see the below timeline for an account of this incident.

—1:30 a.m. Larry heard Mr. Armstrong stirring on the monitor and went up to check on him. Mr. Armstrong had tripped on the box fan in his bathroom and had a very minor cut on his shin. When Larry arrived upstairs he found Mr. Armstrong sitting on the stool in his bathroom. He was coherent and able to communicate that he had tripped on the fan. Larry put a bandage on his shin, removed the box fan and put Mr. Armstrong back in bed.

—4:00 a.m. Larry heard Mr. Armstrong on the monitor again. He went into the restroom and Mr. Armstrong was urinating. He was coherent and able to get back into his bed.

—7:30 a.m. Larry heard Mr. Armstrong again on the monitor and went to check on him. He was using the restroom. Larry got Mr. Armstrong back into bed and made certain he was sleeping.

— 8:30 a.m. Richard arrived and began the morning routine. Larry informed Richard that it had been a difficult night and to please give James his medication and let him sleep in. Richard arrived upstairs and Mr. Armstrong reported that he had an incident and he wanted Richard to stay close to him. Richard gave him his morning leg massage and they began their morning routine. Richard discovered the small scratch on Mr. Armstrong's shin. He did a thorough examination and discovered a scratch and small bump on the back of Mr. Armstrong's head. He asked Mr. Armstrong how this occurred and he could not remember.

When I arrived we all three sat down to discuss the event. Mr. Armstrong could not recall the details of how this occurred.

We went to the bathroom and tried to put the pieces together and could not come up with how, where and when he could have hurt the back of his head.

We spent the rest of the afternoon observing Mr. Armstrong's behavior. Monitoring his thoughts and communication and insuring that this injury was indeed minor. Mr. Armstrong articulated that he did not feel that he needed to see the doctor. We leaned on Richard's expertise and were diligent about our monitoring. After thoughtful consideration and hours of intense observation it was decided that this injury did not require medical attention.

Everyone is very aware that incidents involving the head can be severe and we are continuing our observations of Mr. Armstrong. We will continue to keep a close eye on him. Larry slept in the upstairs bedroom to insure Mr. Armstrong's safety.

Mr. Armstrong has stated this morning that he believes he fell in the shower—though none of the care team sees how this is possible. It's a mystery to all of us how, where and when this event occurred.

James has agreed that an overnight caretaker is something he needs. I have been in touch with Nurses Case Management and we have a candidate available for an interview. I will meet with him ASAP and get him situated down the hall from Mr.

Armstrong during the overnight hours. Larry will continue his diligence in monitoring Mr. Armstrong's nighttime safety until we can get this caregiver in place. Though we are aware that a nighttime caregiver will not fully prevent an incident like this from occurring, we believe that this is a necessary step in Mr. Armstrong's continued care.

Everyone is very grateful that this incident was not more severe. Actions are being taken immediately to make certain that Mr. Armstrong has every opportunity to succeed.

Please feel free to "reply all" to receive the support of this group.

Best,
Nick

Within the next few weeks, Nick was able to interview and select a few candidates for the nighttime caregiver position. It would take two people to fill the position, one working from Sunday through Thursday and the other scheduled for Friday and Saturday evenings. James was able to meet the candidates and selected two of them for the positions. They would begin the following week after spending a day or two with Richard to learn how he worked to meet James' needs. It was a smooth transition. To help James become comfortable with the new routine, I continued going up at night to assist him in getting ready for bed and would go downstairs after he went to sleep. Team Armstrong continued to grow, and after a few weeks, everyone appeared to seamlessly settle into individual routines.

As it turns out, James was not the only one in the house facing some health concerns. During a routine visit with my cardiologist for my annual stress test and checkup, he said I was doing very well, but he brought up an issue with my aortic valve. I knew I had been born with a bicuspid valve (two flaps instead of the normal three), but I assumed everything was OK because I didn't exhibit any symptoms and always did well on the stress test. So I was not prepared when he said he thought it was now time to replace the valve. In discussing the surgery and recovery, he said that they would need to perform open-heart surgery that would require a hospital stay of about a week. Then there would be a six-month recovery period when I would not be able to lift anything or do any activities that would exert any added pressure on my heart. Eventually, I would begin a structured physical therapy program.

I was not ready to hear all of this and knew I could not go through it while being James' primary caregiver. I told him we could not do this now and asked what Plan B would be. He looked at me with kind of a strange expression and said he wasn't asking me if I wanted to do this but telling me that we needed to do this now. There was no Plan B. When I asked what would happen if we didn't go through with this now, he simply replied, "You will die."

Now I was beginning to lose it. I struggled with the idea of how this could be happening now and thought that there had to be another course of action. I guess he could sense that I was not taking this information very well. He told me if I would go visit the surgeon who would be performing the operation, and he told me I could wait; he would support the decision. I was relieved to hear this and was hopeful for a better prognosis. He gave me the contact information, and I left to return home. When I got to the parking lot, I completely lost it and broke down crying. I just couldn't believe this was happening and didn't know how I would get through this. I mean, I have only been in a hospital once in my lifetime, and that was when I had my tonsils removed when I was seven years old. To now have to consider open-heart surgery was just too much to accept, especially in view of everything else that was going on.

The surgeon directed me to get some more tests prior to my appointment. A few weeks later, I met with the surgeon and could not have been more nervous. We talked about what the cardiologist had said to me, and the surgeon asked me what I wanted to do. When I explained my predicament about being a caregiver and needing to postpone this as long as possible, he said he completely understood my concerns. He said he thought I could wait for possibly three to five years, maybe longer, but he wanted me to have regular testing to monitor the size of the hole in my valve. He said once it got to a certain size, we would be out of options and would need to replace the valve. I was relieved to hear his recommendation and asked if he was going to tell my cardiologist. He said he would take care of it, that he had a good working relationship with him, and that everything would be fine. I went home very happy. I decided to keep this information to myself to prevent James from worrying about me, as I wanted to keep the focus on supporting his needs.

It was the end of August 2015 when James surprised me with yet another announcement of a decision he had made without any previous conversations with me. He informed me that he thought we should get married. I was initially stunned because the only time this topic had come up was after some friends got married when he let me know that it would not happen for us, so there was no need to bring it up. I couldn't figure out where this was coming from and why he thought the time was now. But I wasn't going to let this go by without taking action, so that night after our Monday night dinner group met, we asked if our friend, who was a judge, would come by the house. We asked him what the process was for getting married and what steps we needed to take. He informed us that we first needed to get a license from the county, and he told us where we could go the next day to get it. He said that there was supposed to be a three-day waiting period before going to the courthouse for the ceremony with a judge, but it could be waived. He said he would get us on the docket for Wednesday with the judge who was assigned to marriage ceremonies. We told him we did not want to let people know until after the ceremony because we did not want any surprise guests showing up; we just wanted to keep it simple and private with just the two of us in attendance.

We had a regularly scheduled meeting at home the next day with Patti and Jennifer and planned to get the license after they left the house. James was just too excited and happy and could not contain himself; at the end of the meeting, he blurted out that we were getting married the next day. We let them know we were keeping this to ourselves and had not even told our families, planning to call them after the ceremony. They agreed to keep it a secret. We went to the county office and were surprised there weren't any other people there and that we were immediately shown to a clerk, who was able to prepare our license in a matter of minutes.

The next day as we left for the courthouse, Nick and Richard wished us well, and Nick played the song "Going to the Chapel" on his phone. When we arrived at our designated courtroom, there were already about two-dozen people waiting to see the judge for a variety of reasons. I approached the clerk to check in and see where we were on the docket. I gave her our license and went to sit with James as we waited our turn. After a few minutes, the clerk came up to us to say she had spoken with the judge, who knew why we were there. He wanted to let us know he did not perform ceremonies but only signed off on the license and would we be OK with that. We replied that as long as it was legal and official, we were happy.

We were the first ones called up to the bench and introduced ourselves to the judge. He made a few brief comments and asked if we were ready to go through with the marriage. He then performed his duties and pronounced us married, and said we could go ahead and kiss each other if we wanted. But we said we were OK since we had been together for over thirty years; it wasn't necessary. We turned to go out of the courtroom, and when I got to the exit, I turned around and saw that James had stopped in front of the group waiting in the courtroom and proudly announced that we had just gotten married. There was a rousing round of applause.

When we got home, James called each of his children, and I called my family members to share the wonderful news. Everyone seemed very pleased and congratulated us with much enthusiasm. I found it interesting, though, that when James was talking to Brad and Liz, he said that he wanted them to be happy for us; he didn't use this phrase with anyone else. This led me to believe that James was well aware of how I was being treated by them and that his decision to get married now was just one more way he could protect me. To celebrate, we took Nick and his husband to dinner with us at one of our favorite restaurants. The staff found out what we were celebrating and prepared a beautiful dessert to congratulate us.

Over the next week, we sent out numerous e-mails to our friends to share our good news and received so many congratulatory notes. We heard some rumors that people were talking about throwing us a reception. We decided to get a step ahead of them and planned a party ourselves. James' eightieth birthday party was intended to be our last big event, so we decided on a smaller reception for no more than 150 of our Austin friends. We decided to host the reception in ZACH Theatre's lobby, with a variety of food stations and a few bars. Instead of a cake, we chose to have individual cupcakes on display. Along with numerous flower displays would be a scattering of tables and chairs throughout the lobby. We asked ZACH to provide a few of their artists to perform a couple of musical numbers for the entertainment. Our favorite caterer and florist collaborated with the theatre's event planner so everyone would be on the same page. Though it was extremely hot the day of the reception, everyone showed up to celebrate with us, and we had a wonderful time.

A special family meeting was held a few weeks after the ceremony with the administrators, lawyer, and accountant to discuss how our marriage changed some of the estate planning paperwork, the will, and the preparation of future tax filings. One of the major changes was that now my trust and inheritance would pass to me tax-free, saving a sizable amount of money for both the estate and me. Also, filing our taxes as married would be financially beneficial to James. Our getting married was one of the best decisions we ever made. At the time, we had no idea that it would positively impact us in so many ways.

We maintained a fairly active social calendar that included going out to dinner almost every night mixed in with dinner parties, receptions, theatre shows, fund-raisers, and the occasional concert. One night we were invited to a friend's home for a salon concert with a quartet from the university's music school. After the cocktail reception, the guests were guided into the beautifully decorated living room to get settled for the concert portion of the evening. James and I were seated behind our hosts and having a wonderful time. When the concert ended, our host, who was about James' age, rose to say a few words, and I noticed he seemed to struggle while getting up from his chair and looked like he was about to fall. Without thinking, I jumped up to try to steady him, but he was much bigger and was too far off balance and began to fall. All I could think of was to try and break his fall and guide him to land on top of me. Other guests quickly got up to assist us and were able to get him to his feet. Fortunately, he was fine and hadn't hurt himself, but I was not so lucky. When I tried to get up, a sharp pain shot up my right leg that was almost unbearable. Because the guests were still focused on our host, I was able to step away to try and walk it off, thinking I'd probably just pulled something. But any time I placed weight on the leg, the pain almost brought me to tears. Somehow I was able to bear it long enough to get through the buffet dinner before finally getting to go home. I was able to help James get ready for bed and quickly went to my room to do the same and to get off of my feet.

I was able to sleep through the night, but when I got up in the morning and stood up, the pain almost knocked me off my feet. Now I knew it was more than a pulled muscle, and I had to take action. I called my sports medicine doctor to see if I could get in to see him that day. I explained my situation and said he had to do something to help relieve the pain. I had been to him a number of times before when I'd hurt myself, and he was always able to get me back to normal. After my initial exam, which included moving my leg in various positions and determining where the pain originated, he wasn't sure what I had damaged but said he would begin a treatment regimen until I could get an MRI to determine what was going on.

I went in a few days later for more treatment and was face down on the table when the assistant walked in and asked if I had seen the bruise on the back of my leg, which went from my hip to my knee. I said I hadn't, and he said he had to get the doctor to look at it because it was quite remarkable. I was certain he had seen plenty of bruises before, and it couldn't have been that bad. But then the doctor came in, looked at my leg, and said he had to take pictures for his website because it was the worst one he had ever seen. Once I finished my treatment, which was definitely working because the pain wasn't as severe, the assistant put a lot of strips of tape on my leg for support, and I was able to go home.

It took a few weeks to get my MRI scheduled due to insurance issues, so it was a full three weeks after the incident that I was able to finally bring the results to my doctor. After reviewing the report, he said he thought I needed surgery because I apparently had torn 90 percent of my hamstring. When I asked what would be involved, I was discouraged. My recovery period would involve about six months of not placing any stress on my right leg while it was healing. There would also be a long process of physical therapy to help prevent scar tissue from forming. I told him about being a primary caregiver and that I couldn't possibly go through with this procedure. Was there any other option? He didn't think so but said I should consult with an orthopedic surgeon to see what he would say. Fortunately, our neighbor was an orthopedic surgeon, and I shared my report with him. He said that because I was relatively young, not doing extreme exercise, and wasn't in pain, I could opt out of the surgery, continue with the therapy sessions, and I would probably recover in a few months. When I shared this with my sports medicine doctor, he agreed to help me, and after a few months of treatment, everything was fine.

Every once in a while, something unexpected would happen to James that would catch us off guard because it was a first-time incident. Nick did a good job of summarizing one such incident with the following report, sent out on November 11, 2015:

Armstrong Family,

I write to keep you informed of an issue that occurred this morning in the Armstrong/Connelly residence. Mr. Armstrong had a normal, low-key evening at home with Larry. They had dinner at home and Mr. Armstrong and Larry got to bed at the usual hour.

Edward showed up at his normal time for the overnight shift.

Mr. Armstrong was in bed and asleep at 10:28 p.m. At 5:27 a.m. he woke up to use the restroom. Edward was there to assist him. He immediately fell back asleep and slept until 7:15 a.m. At 7:15 a.m. he woke up and used the restroom again. Edward was there to assist him.

Richard arrived at 8:15 a.m. to begin his shift. Edward reported to Richard that it was a normal evening for Mr. Armstrong. Over the past few months of overnight care Mr. Armstrong has really improved his sleeping. He only wakes up once or twice during the nighttime hours to use the restroom.

Richard went to wake Mr. Armstrong at 9:10 a.m. Mr. Armstrong was snoring heavily and in a deep sleep. Richard attempted to wake him verbally (which is his standard morning routine). Mr. Armstrong was not responding to Richard's voice. Richard was comforted by Mr. Armstrong's strong and steady breath/snoring but still was uncertain as to why Mr. Armstrong was not responding.

Richard used a stronger voice in hopes of waking Mr. Armstrong from a deep sleep. Richard then began trying to wake him with physical touch. Mr. Armstrong was not responding to Richard's physical attempts to wake him up either. It was clear that his breathing was steady and deep. Richard decided to alert Larry and get his assistance.

I arrived at the home at this point. Larry and I went upstairs to attempt to wake Mr. Armstrong from this heavy sleep. He was snoring and breathing as though he was in a very deep sleep. He was not responding to our voices or our touch.

Larry made the decision that the ambulance needed to be dispatched to the house. The fire department showed up first. The technician was able to wake Mr. Armstrong with a firm massage to the chest area. Mr. Armstrong opened his eyes and was able to articulate that he needed to use the restroom. His speech was slow and muddy. The technician from the fire department requested that he stay seated on the edge of the bed until the emergency medical staff arrived. They arrived within moments and began running a series of tests. They tested his blood sugar, blood pressure, heart rate, breathing, and conducted a test that ruled out a stroke.

Mr. Armstrong tested completely normal on all these tests. The EMS deemed him stable and suggested that he be taken to the hospital for further testing. He left the home in an ambulance at 10:15 a.m.

Mr. Armstrong was taken to Seton hospital where they did blood tests, X-rays, CT scans, chest X-ray. He tested normal on all of these tests and was released at 2:30 p.m. Mr. Armstrong and Larry were sent home with information on care for Altered Level of Consciousness (ALOC). This is basic information for anyone who has had a change in level of alertness. The entire care team will familiarize themselves with this information. The majority of the information in the packet is procedure that our care team does on a daily basis.

The doctors requested that he follow up with his general practitioner and his neurologist. He will see his GP tomorrow.

Mr. Armstrong was not able to eat, drink or take his medications until after he was released from the hospital. Larry cooked him a large meal and administered his medication as soon as they got home. Mr. Armstrong is currently resting in his chair and watching a movie.

I will keep everyone informed if anything is discovered over next few days. Please feel free to contact me with any questions or concerns you might have. As always, you can press "reply all" to receive the support of this group.

Best,
Nick

We enjoyed a quiet holiday season, though we still went to pick out our usual oversized Christmas tree and invited friends over for a holiday party at the beginning of December. But it was becoming common for James to develop a persistent cough that had the potential to cause pneumonia. The first couple of years this happened, James would respond well to cough medicine and antibiotics prescribed by our PCP. But this year, it seemed worse, and after a few weeks, there was no improvement, and breathing became more difficult for James. Our doctor recommended that we take James to the ER for treatment, and they discovered fluid building up in his lungs and decided to have him admitted for treatment. This would cause a minor shake-up for the household team, with the caregivers all doing their shifts at the hospital, including me on the dinner-to-bedtime and all-day Sunday shift. James had a complicated medicine schedule requiring certain pills to be given four different times during the day. This schedule was developed over many years, and we knew that if we didn't maintain it, James would be "off" mentally, along with having coordination issues. Receiving his medications on time allowed James to be at his strongest, to successfully maintain his daily routines, and to show few signs of having Parkinson's. Re-creating this schedule at the hospital was difficult because of the rotation of different nurses. We opted to have a caregiver on duty at all times to help monitor the medications. We maintained a binder with multiple copies of James' medication schedule and were able to check off the meds once they had been given to James. The nurses were very supportive of our routine and happily cooperated with us. It took almost two weeks of treatment before James was able to safely return home.

A few months later, while we were performing our usual bedtime routine, we had a major incident that we'd worried about and tried our best to prevent. While standing at the bathroom sink, James turned to walk over to his dressing area, where I was preparing his bedtime clothes. As he turned, his foot caught on the carpet, and he lost his balance and fell. Fortunately, I was standing right there, and the nighttime caregiver was upstairs in his area preparing for the evening. It didn't look like a bad fall since it was on carpeting, and James did not hit his head on any of the bathroom fixtures. I checked him over to see if there was any pain, but James said he thought he was fine. When I helped him up to sit on a nearby stool, James said he felt some pain in his leg. I called for the caregiver to join us, and after re-evaluating James' condition, we decided to call EMS to check him out. They arrived within a few minutes, and after assessing James' condition, they didn't think anything was broken but determined he should go to the ER for X-rays just to make sure there wasn't a fracture. James agreed with their assessment, so while they prepared to take James, I gathered up his medications and a few toiletries just in case he was admitted to the hospital. I followed them to the hospital and met them in the ER. It was after 11:00 p.m. by the time we were able to see a doctor who would review James' X-rays. About an hour later, the doctor came back to inform us that James had a hip fracture that would require a partial hip replacement. There was a surgery team on duty, but when we met with the surgeon, he suggested that since it was so late, we wait until the morning when he would have his usual support staff on duty that would be fresh to assist with the surgery. I mentioned that James had Parkinson's and still hadn't had his nighttime meds and that I hoped he could take them because it would be late the next day before he would be able to take them again. Since the pharmacy was closed for the night, they allowed me to give him his most important meds and then took him up to a room to prepare him for the evening. Once he was settled in for the night, the caregiver stayed in James' room, and I went home to get some sleep knowing the next day was going to be long.

Richard arrived at the hospital in the morning to relieve the night-time caregiver and begin his shift. When I arrived, Richard was in the waiting room because James was still in surgery. It was a few hours before I was informed that James was out of surgery. I spoke with the surgeon, who said that everything had gone well and that James would stay in the recovery area for a while before returning to his room, where I could see him. James' mother had had hip surgery, so we had a good idea of what the recovery process would look like. Fortunately, she responded well to her therapy and eventually was able to walk again, and we were hoping for the same results for James. James had had two knee-replacement surgeries, so he was familiar with the kind of recovery process that was in store for him.

The surgery and recovery prevented James from following his medication schedule for a day, and it took a couple of days for him to become alert and coherent, be able to clearly communicate, and feel well enough to eat. After about ten days, James was discharged and sent to a rehab facility to begin his physical therapy treatment. The caregivers and I continued our rotation schedule so James would always have someone with him to monitor his progress, learn some of the treatment techniques used to help James, and assist him when there was no rehab staff in his room.

James maintained a fairly positive attitude during all of this, though he would remain in this facility for weeks before they would allow him to go home. Along with overseeing James' care, I was monitoring work projects at El Greco and checking in with the renovation progress at Scenic, which was on schedule but still a few months from completion. Nick had recently had to leave his job, so it was up to me to maintain projects at both of our residences. We had been trying our hardest to keep James safe at home and were hoping he would make it to Scenic before something like this happened. We were now more certain than ever that James had made the right decision to create a home where he could function more comfortably and safely. I mentioned to the construction manager that James would soon return home, but before they would release him, I needed to have a ramp installed at our front gate, where we had two steps, so James could be wheeled into the house. He said they would take care of it, and by the next afternoon, they had a ramp constructed complete with a handrail ready for James' return home.

Returning home to El Greco in a wheelchair would prove to be challenging. The hall to the bathroom that James frequently used was very narrow, leaving no room to turn the wheelchair and very little space to maneuver around the chair to assist James. Washing his hands also proved to be nearly impossible because it was so difficult to reach the faucet while in a wheelchair. Though we had an elevator to transport James up to the master suite, it was barely large enough for the wheelchair and didn't leave enough room for the caregiver to travel with James. When James was in his bathroom preparing for bed or getting ready in the morning, he had to sit with his side to the sink, making it difficult to brush his teeth or shave. These are only some of the challenges which emphasized the importance of moving to Scenic, which was being designed with James' needs in mind. There would be no steps, and there would be easy access to the bathrooms, including having a roll-in shower and openings under all the sinks for James to easily reach the faucet and see himself in the mirror when seated in his wheelchair. But we still had a few months before the house would be ready for us to move in. We would have to make due with the current situation.

The professional organizer continued to help us prepare for the move to Scenic. She began on the top floor with James' master suite, going through closets and storage areas to help James choose items he was comfortable getting rid of and organizing everything else into various moving containers. James seemed to enjoy this process because he was able to reminisce about photos and other items that he hadn't seen in years. We had lived in El Greco for twenty-five years, and he hadn't gotten rid of anything during that time. If she thought this area had been challenging, she would soon find out the library was going to be where James was most resistant to downsizing. In the end, I don't believe she was able to convince James to get rid of anything, which resulted in over fifty boxes of items to move to the new house from the library alone.

The kitchen was the next area to conquer. Since there was an amazing amount of storage, we never got rid of anything over the years. Along with about a dozen complete sets of china, there were numerous sets of silverware and glassware, as well as multiple serving pieces in silver, crystal, and china. But James didn't want to let go of any of these items. The organizer was able to go through the drawers and identify many duplicates of various utensils that we agreed to let go of, along with some individual glasses and dishes that were not pieces of any sets.

We continued this process for the next few months. We felt it was completely worthwhile and helpful for preparing for the move, which was quickly approaching. Since our renovation crew was doing an excellent job of remaining on the schedule, we felt comfortable scheduling the movers and setting the move-in date. When we met with a representative of the moving company, he determined it would take four days to pack everything up, and the actual move-in process would take two days. He was agreeable to moving our two bedroom sets and some library furniture on day one and everything else on the second day. This way, we could move James in, and he would be settled at Scenic when they began moving everything over on the second day.

We had a separate company move all the artwork on day one; they also installed some of the major pieces. They would return the following week to install the rest of the pieces after we were more settled. Though our contractor warned us about moving too fast, since he had to get an inspection approved for us to take up occupancy, we decided it was worth the risk and hoped there would be no unexpected delays.

Everything seemed to be going well until we were presented with two challenges. James' daughter, Liz, informed us that Brad's younger son would be playing in a baseball tournament about an hour and a half from Austin the same week we would be moving. She wanted to coordinate various times when they might come down to visit or maybe have lunch or dinner with James. I told her that I would not be available to help her with the planning because I would have my hands full coordinating the packing and move-in process; she would need to coordinate directly with James. I said I could provide her with her dad's schedule for that week and that she could coordinate any visits or meals with her dad, but to please not involve me. Though she tried to challenge me on this, I told her I was confident she could figure it out on her own.

The other issue was that when we went to James' scheduled visit with his cardiologist, he said he thought James might need an additional stent or two and scheduled James to go to the hospital for further testing. After the doctor reviewed the results, he came to our room and informed us that James was doing well and he would not need the procedure. During this visit, he also started talking about my condition that I still hadn't shared with James. I wanted to wait until I had to have the operation and didn't want to concern James. Seeing me vigorously shaking my head, he quickly understood the situation and went in a different direction, talking about releasing James to go home. As I walked out with him, we stopped in the hallway, and he profusely apologized for almost spilling the beans. He understood why I hadn't shared this information with James. Disaster averted.

Moving day was quickly approaching, with only a few days more to get ready. I made some final preparations, packing things too delicate for the movers to handle and preparing overnight bags for James and me for our first night at Scenic. When the movers arrived on Monday to begin packing us up, I walked through the house with the manager and showed him our boxed toiletries, the suitcases with our clothes for the week, the towels hanging in the bathroom, and the cupboard in the kitchen that we asked them to leave alone; everything else could be packed up. I watched in amazement as they went through the house, filling one box after another, creating stacks of cardboard boxes in every room. I hadn't realized until now that I would be responsible for unpacking all of this in a few days since my focus had solely been on the packing and moving processes. Over the next few days, I also coordinated with the audio people, who would move and set up our televisions and stereo equipment, the art specialists who were going to move the art and hang the larger pieces, and the renovation team, who were working overtime to meet our move-in deadline in just three days. It was becoming a daunting task, but I was pleased by how well it all was working out, and I was glad that we still had the organizer with us to take on some of the responsibilities. It helped that we were moving only three blocks away and that the weather was holding up for us. We hadn't worked with this moving company or the art specialists before, but they were doing an exceptional job and were so accommodating to our needs that I was feeling very little pressure.

On the first day of our move, the movers packed up the major pieces in our two bedrooms and a couple of furniture pieces for the library, where we would station James for the day. The art specialists arrived to take all of the artwork out of the house and move it to Scenic, where they would hang about two dozen of the major pieces and store the rest for a later date when they would return to complete their work. I went over to Scenic while our organizer remained behind to supervise and met the construction manager, who assured me he had the permit for us to move forward and I could let the movers in with the first load of furniture. When they went back to El Greco to finish packing, we brought James over and settled him in the library, where he awaited the arrival of the art. When the art specialists arrived later that afternoon, they sorted out the paintings we wanted to be installed that day in the living room and stored all of the other pieces on the lower level, where they would be out of the way. James and I had already decided where we wanted these pieces placed. Since there was very little furniture and they were the only people in the house, they were able to move very quickly.

It was getting dark as they finished their work, so we had all of the lights on in the house. James had the biggest smile on his face when he rolled into the living room and saw how much better his art looked under these conditions. There was no furniture in the living room, so it felt like we were in an art gallery. This was a huge space. For the first time, he could see the larger pieces from a distance, and the improved lighting made the art look almost new. He spent the next hour moving from piece to piece, admiring the art like he was seeing it for the first time. Everything we had gone through to get to this point was worth it just to see him enjoying this moment. It was difficult, but eventually, I got James to go to his bedroom and get ready for bed. Tomorrow was going to be another big day filled with excitement as we began our next chapter by moving into our new house.

We got up early because we didn't know when they were going to begin delivering the rest of our belongings. I went over to El Greco to let the movers in and get an estimate as to when they would begin heading over to Scenic with the first load. Our organizer arrived, and when the first truck was getting ready to leave, I followed them to Scenic, and she remained behind to supervise. We were now in the midst of a major juggling act trying to determine the best placement for everything. Including not only the furniture, but all of the packed boxes, which was at a number I was not prepared for as they were arriving in what appeared to be a never-ending stream of cardboard. Along with the main floor, which was made up of the kitchen, dining room, foyer, living room, library, and two master suites, we had two bedrooms and a family room one floor below and a maid's apartment above the three-car garage. At some point during the day, James' family, visiting for the baseball game, stopped by for a visit and to see the house now that it was finished. A few friends in the neighborhood also popped in to add to the excitement and chaos. But all of this activity helped keep James occupied, so he didn't have to focus on everything else that was going on. The audio-visual people arrived that afternoon to begin installing everything after going to El Greco to get all of the TVs and stereo equipment. Now James would have TV to watch and be able to play his favorite records. One surprise during all of the activity was that our construction manager, who knew James loved watching TV, brought us a new large-screen TV for the library, which was the perfect house-warming gift. The contractor said he was pleased to do it; he said this was the first house he'd worked on that had an actual purpose for the owner—to accommodate his specific needs.

Much later that day, after everyone was gone, I walked through the house to begin developing a plan of attack on where to begin the unpacking process. Aside from the fifty boxes from the library currently stacked in the living room, I was taken aback when I went to the garage to find over three hundred boxes stacked at least eight feet high, filling all three car stalls. I wasn't keeping track, but whenever they brought in a box, and I wasn't sure where to place it, I said to put it in the garage. I had no idea it would amount to this many boxes and determined this would be the last place where I would work, focusing first on what was already inside the house.

I decided to work on James' bedroom first to make sure he was comfortable and had access to everything he needed. While I did this, our organizer started in the kitchen, which I knew would take the longest time since we had gone through this process once before when we renovated the El Greco kitchen. After James' room, I worked on my bedroom, which didn't take very long. I went to help out in the kitchen, which took a few more days. Then there was the library, which had all of those boxes waiting to be unpacked. Though our architect had done a beautiful job of creating a full wall of bookcases, it was about half the space we had at El Greco, so we had a major organizational task ahead of us. We first sorted the books by categories such as art, cars, history, travel, and so on. Then we got James involved to decide which books he wanted on display and which ones could be placed into various cabinets and other rooms throughout the house. This task was a lot more difficult than I anticipated; it took us a full week to complete this challenge.

I hadn't thought about the accumulation of all of the empty boxes and packing paper; how did one get rid of them? The organizer suggested I call our mover to see if we could pay him to come by once a week to pick these items up and dispose of them for us. I was pleased to find out he was agreeable to helping us, and this arrangement worked out very well for us. Finally, it was time to tackle the mountain of boxes in the garage. The boxes weren't organized by category, so I just began in the car stall at one end and slowly moved across the garage. Since we had a ramp installed in the garage to easily get James down to his car, I began on that end to create the access he needed. It was a slow process; I plodded along one day at a time.

I don't know what caused James to think of it, but one day he asked me about his two large pieces of malachite. He wanted to see them. I said I was sure they were in a box in the garage, but there was no way of determining exactly where they were, and he would just have to be patient. He never asked about anything else—just the malachite. He would bring it up every three or four days. I finally brought him out to the garage so he could see the amount of boxes I was dealing with, but he persisted. He wanted to see those malachite pieces. To this day, I still don't believe that after another three weeks of working in the garage, I opened the very last box, and there, on the bottom, were the two malachite pieces. I happily brought the box into the library and opened it in front of James, presenting him with his precious rocks. I found a place in the living room where he would be able to see them every day from his library chair.

Moving to Scenic proved to be one of the best decisions James had ever made. After months of struggling to manipulate a wheelchair at El Greco, moving around the Scenic house was so much easier for James and his caregivers. He was able to roll up to his sink in his bathroom while getting ready, able to be easily rolled into his shower and seated on a bench while bathing, and the bathroom next to his chair in the library was large enough for him to move around in his wheelchair and easily access the sink and see into the mirror without any issues. With all of the improved lighting and increased space, James' artwork had never looked so good. James even mentioned that it was like seeing it all new again. All of this was not possible at El Greco. Now James could accomplish tasks more independently, which made him feel so much better. The move also had a positive impact on the caregivers, as all of these conveniences made their jobs much more manageable and less stressful.

James now began socializing more. He enjoyed showing off the new house, and we were hosting dinner parties again, including an event for two hundred people to benefit our regional theatre. We also invited a large group of friends and neighbors over for an open house. We had to cancel the first open house date as James had his coughing issue again and was hospitalized for a few weeks, so it wasn't until May 2017 that we were able to reschedule it. We had two unexpected positive outcomes from our party. One was when we invited the family who had built and previously lived in our house to come to the party. The second was when we had the first neighborhood party for people who lived within a block of our home, many who had never met before since they too had recently moved into the neighborhood.

The previous owners were initially taken aback by the significant changes we had made, going from a very traditional home that was darker with a lot of wood trim to a highly contemporary design that was light, with clean lines to showcase the art. In the end, we received a positive response, and they seemed pleased with the results. During the party, James decided to sit at a table with four chairs that were near the center of the living room. Throughout the evening, guests would rotate sitting at the table to visit with James. He loved talking about the renovation and answering questions about various pieces of his art collection. The party went on for many hours due to our neighbors having such a good time meeting each other and discovering many common interests. One neighbor said she wanted to create regularly scheduled neighborhood get-togethers that would rotate the party from house to house on our block, which we were pleased to have initiated with our open house.

James continued his physical therapy throughout the summer, but it was getting more difficult for him due to low blood pressure, so we moved the therapy to the house rather than going to the out-patient clinic. It was just a few months prior that he was doing well enough to walk from his bedroom to the kitchen each morning using a walker. We were also able to walk into a few restaurants using a walker, which achieved James' long-term goal of me not having to bring the wheelchair with us each time we went out to dinner. Though it was becoming more difficult to do the therapy, James persisted because he had been able to accomplish walking in the past.

We continued going out to dinner almost every night, including our long-standing Monday Night Dinners with a set of friends that could total up to as many as nine people. We went to a Chinese restaurant one Monday night, but only three other friends were able to join us. It was actually nice having a smaller group, as it was easier to take turns talking and listening to each other. James was very animated that night, and we had a great time. We went out to the parking lot to say our usual goodbyes, but as I was assisting James in getting into the car, I could tell something wasn't quite right. I thought he was possibly having issues with his blood pressure and quickly determined that I needed to get him to a nearby fire department, where an EMS team could assist him.

One of our friends got into the backseat to go with us, and his partner took the other friend home and waited for our call to let him know what was going on. As we left the restaurant, I remembered that there was an ER at a hospital just up the road and decided to go there. Fortunately, it was later in the evening, so there wasn't much traffic, and we were able to travel quickly. When we arrived at the ER, there was a nurse outside who went in to get a doctor to check on James. When the doctor was checking out James, he asked me, "Do you realize he has stopped breathing?" I was stunned and felt like I had been punched in the stomach; I couldn't believe what I was hearing. I had held James' hand all the way to the hospital, and it was still warm, so I was certain he would be OK once he received some oxygen. He never said anything during the ride, but I thought back to when I helped him into the car. At one point, he looked me in the eye and had the strangest look on his face. Almost like he was smiling, and his eyes had a special twinkle, but I hadn't paid much attention to it at that moment.

I quickly returned to the present and heard the doctor asking me if James had a "do not resuscitate" order (DNR). I said yes and that I had medical power of attorney. He then asked me if I wanted them to try and resuscitate him or honor the DNR. At first, I wanted them to try and revive him because I still couldn't believe this was happening. But then I remembered James making me promise that I would never let them put him on a respirator. He always regretted doing it to his mother and watching how difficult it was for her. When we were completing the paperwork to document James' wishes with our nurse from Nurse Case Management, she made a point of making sure I would be able to make this decision when the time came. So I told them no. He said that they would prepare him inside the ER and then come and get me so I could see him one last time. I still could not believe what was happening and was having a very difficult time processing what I needed to do next.

My friend called his husband and asked him to come to the hospital. When he arrived, I asked if they would call James' kids; I was in no condition to talk to anyone. After they made those calls, I said we needed to contact the nighttime caregiver to let him know he wouldn't have to come to work that night because James "was in the hospital," and I would stay with him tonight and would get back to him tomorrow with more details. I wanted to let his supervisor, Debbie, know first so she could take care of notifying all of the NCM staff who worked with us. I wasn't sure how they handled situations like this.

The doctor let me in to see James. This was probably the worst thing I had ever experienced. Though James looked so peaceful, I was devastated and still not completely accepting what was happening. I sat next to him for a long time, holding his hand and thanking him for everything he had done for me, basically providing me with such a wonderful life. I removed his wedding ring and placed it on my right hand so I would always have a piece of him with me. At that point, the shock was wearing off, and I completely broke down. After some minutes had passed, I was having difficulty breathing and went outside for some fresh air. I found a bench to sit down on and kept thinking over and over again about what was happening. I needed to see our good friends Rusty and Mary. I called them. Rusty answered and asked what was going on. I told him what had happened. He asked where I was and told me that they were on their way.

After a short time passed, Rusty and Mary arrived. When they approached me, I completely broke down again. For quite a while, I was unable to control myself or to provide them with more details. At this point, I asked if they wanted to see James, which they did. During this time, the head ER doctor asked to see me and took me aside. He started asking questions about James and my relationship and then went in a direction for which I wasn't prepared. He asked about my emotional and mental state and whether I was on any special medications. He then led me into symptoms of depression and gave me advice on what to do if I developed any of them. This conversation went on for about thirty minutes, as he was quite thorough and wanted to make sure I could take care of myself.

At some point later, we decided to leave. A friend said he would drive me, and everyone else would follow us to the house. I opened the door to let them in and noticed the lights were still on at our friend's house across the street. I told the group to go in and that I would be back in a few minutes. I knocked on the door. Chris answered and could tell something was wrong. When I told him James was gone, I lost it again. He comforted me and called for his wife to come down. We sat down, and I told them the whole story. I wanted them to know because I was unsure of what the next few weeks would entail, and I wanted them to be prepared. I think they appreciated the heads-up, and I returned to my friends at home.

We met in the kitchen and decided to open some wine to toast James and his extraordinary life. After sharing some of our favorite memories, Mary decided she would stay the night because she didn't want me to be alone. Another friend would stay the next night. They would continue this for as long as I needed. I tried to stop them, but they were determined. After everyone left, I took Mary down to the guest room, and I went to my room to get ready for bed.

I don't know what time I woke up, but Mary was already in the kitchen. After eating, I decided I needed to call my family. One of my sisters said she would get a flight and visit me the rest of the week. By this time, Mary said I needed to see what was going on around town and showed me what was happening on Facebook. Already, there were numerous posts about James, which I couldn't believe because I did not follow Facebook and didn't know how people were finding out so quickly or how fast the news was spreading all over town.

There are too many posts to include here, but I want to share one from Dave, the Artistic Director at ZACH Theatre, who said it best:

I love you JAMES ARMSTRONG

Without James …

… there is no Topfer Theatre.

… there was no glorious Opening Production of Ragtime.

… there wasn't a Karen Kuykendall Stage at ZACH.

…there weren't scholarships for kids who couldn't afford theatre classes.

…there isn't ANN starring Holland Taylor on our stage to remind of the values we expect from elected officials and that "we" are the people.

…there isn't an orchestra for Sunday in the Park With George.

…there weren't Pre-Professional students pursuing their dream of a life and career in the arts.

…there aren't three queens in fabulous frocks making their way across the Outback spreading Pride, Love, and Acceptance.

… Anna never gets to take that dance with the King with 50 Asian American actors onstage, lifting our hearts with a catch in our throat as she lifted her skirt to waltz.

… there weren't busloads of school kids coming to ZACH to see bilingual plays in our Theatre for Families program.

… there's no Frog and Toad to teach us values of true friendship.

…there weren't students in the College-bound Conservatory who didn't have the resources for this college preparation.

… and that's the thing about the proverbial iceberg. The thing about James is that he always came on board every initiative, every idea, every opportunity FIRST——do you know how significant that is to a group like ZACH? The trust and belief in that is overwhelming and so appreciated. Think of the impact he has had across our city in numerous arts organizations, and hospitals, and social service organizations, and gay culture and rights organizations, and charities large and small, and the list goes on and on … just like this man's compassion and heart and intellect and wit and expansiveness.

Unforgettable in every way, that's what you are. Godspeed dearest soul.

I love you James Armstrong.

A few days later, my sister arrived, which greatly helped me out. She was able to help answer phone calls, greet friends who were stopping by the house to pay their respects, and help me begin organizing James' Celebration of Life ceremony. Brad and Patti got things started by reviewing notes from a visit James and I had made to a funeral home to make some preliminary decisions about what James would want to happen when the time came. They also narrowed the date to September 15 or 16 and began researching some of the venues discussed at the funeral home visit for availability. But to my surprise, I received a phone call from a good friend who worked at Ballet Austin who said they were willing to offer the Performing Arts Center on the 15th because they had it reserved that weekend for their season opener and could make it available earlier in the day. This would include the use of a beautiful backdrop on the stage for their production of Romeo and Juliet. This was absolutely incredible and would be perfect because this was the home of the opera, symphony, and ballet performances and numerous events we had attended for so many years. And due to our donation to the capital campaign to build the complex, our names were significantly displayed on the main staircase. This just brought the Celebration of Life to a new level of production. I had a lot of work ahead of me, and it would take a large contingent of friends to make it happen.

Chapter 9

REMEMBERING JAMES

*L*iving alone at Scenic was not an easy transition. As stated in the Marriage Trust, I was to be allowed to remain in the home at no cost to me for a minimum of six months or until it sold. But every time I went from my bedroom to the kitchen, I expected to see James sitting in his chair in the library, where we spent most of our time together. I was not able to go back into the library anymore and spent the majority of my time in my bedroom, the kitchen, and my office downstairs. I had James' memorial service to plan, which gave me a purpose to forge ahead through the mourning process.

Leave it to Liz to provide the first bump in the road, when she sent an e-mail a few days after the new venue for the memorial was announced questioning why we couldn't have the service on Saturday the 16th, even though there was a community event planned outside the performing arts center that day. She seemed convinced that parking could not be the issue since the parking garage was designed with multiple events in mind.

I wished Liz knew as much as she thought she did. First of all, the ballet said we could have the venue on Friday the 15th before they had to make final preparations for their performance that evening. They were also going to provide seats in two boxes for opening night, one for my family and one for the Armstrong family, and were going to dedicate that night's performance to James' memory. Then there is the parking garage, which was not built large enough to handle multiple events for the Long Center and the Palmer Event Center next door due to height restrictions established by the neighborhood. Traffic would also be an issue if there were a community-wide event happening at the same time we were attempting to have a service for James. There were just too many issues making a Saturday service very difficult, so I sent this quick reply, hoping it would end further discussion about the choice of date, and I could continue with the planning process:

> The Ballet folks said it will be an open community event with thousands of kids and families and all of the parking garages will be full for most of the morning and afternoon. We wouldn't have any access to parking and there could be issues with traffic and access into the building. Friday has absolutely no issues or barriers.
>
> Larry

This seemed to appease Liz, and the family communication going forward was positive and supportive. They gave me free rein to do whatever I thought was needed and gave me no budget restrictions. Since we were now going to be at the Long Center, I decided to stay with a theme of highlighting the various arts organizations James and I had supported for so many years. I first made calls to my contacts at the opera, symphony, and ballet to see if they could help me select a speaker from their organization who would make a few remarks about James and then introduce a representative to do a short performance. I then asked the Artistic Director at ZACH, Dave, if he would help organize the service and act as the master of ceremonies and introduce everyone at the appointed time. Also, since I didn't have any production experience, I asked if he would help communicate with the Long Center staff that would be working the day of the service. I also asked for a ZACH performance to open the service and another one to close the service. He was happy to help out, and with his involvement, I knew we were going to have a service of superior quality.

My next call was to the Director of the Armstrong Community Music School to see if she would speak and introduce someone from the school to perform. She said she would be honored and would begin working on something very special to honor James. My next call was to a member of a classical quartet James helped support to bring to the university to see if they would be available. Unfortunately, some of their members would be out of town, but he would check on a new quartet at the university we had recently heard perform and really liked. A few days later, he got back to me with the good news that they would be honored to perform and gave me their contact information to make final arrangements. The Dean of the College of Fine Arts would introduce them at the ceremony. Now I felt like I had all of my bases covered. Or, so I thought.

I don't remember who first mentioned it, but I was asked if I had given thought to creating a photo slideshow to play before the service began as people were entering the venue. I said I hadn't and had no idea of how to create one or the amount of work it would take. Dave mentioned a video designer currently working on a project at ZACH who might be able to help, but it turned out that she would not be in Austin. Some friends said they knew someone who had done a slideshow before and that they would work with him to create one. I spent the next few days gathering up as many photos as I could and handed them over for them to do the rest of the work.

A few years before, James had hired a videographer who interviewed James about his life and created a four-hour video that we gave to each of James' children and his granddaughter. He contacted me to ask if I would like to show a condensed version of the interview at the service. He said if I gave him the time restriction, he could create something for me to review to see if I wanted to include it. I said I would be interested and gave him the information he needed, along with a deadline of when it needed to be complete.

Another key player to help me organize everything was my friend at the ballet, Pei San, who went above the call of duty to ensure that everything would go smoothly. She called one day to say she had received a call from the mayor's office asking if I had contacted them to see if the mayor would speak at the memorial. This was the only major glitch that I had somehow overlooked, and I was completely embarrassed by my oversight. I asked Pei San if the mayor wanted to participate, and she said he was very interested; she volunteered to call his office to make the necessary arrangements. As it turned out, he would be heading to the airport late the morning of the service but would come by to say a few words. We would have to be fluid with the schedule and insert him whenever he arrived. We had known the mayor for many years and were good friends, and it was going to be a huge honor to have him speak at the service. Everyone stepped up their game to make it happen, including the Long Center staff that arranged special access for the mayor to the auditorium through the backstage area.

Working with David, our favorite florist and event planner, has always been a joy. He was also taking on a lot of the planning, especially coordinating with the funeral home and the Long Center's food service staff. He came over to discuss how best to set up everything at the Long Center, from tables for people to sign memorial books to how best to set the stage. The lectern would be on one side and on the other side a display of flowers, the large painting of James and me that was done for the opera gala honoring James, and the urn containing his ashes. David brought a bouquet of flowers to show what colors he wanted to use and to make sure he was including some of James' favorites. He went over the menu for the reception and showed me how the food tables and bars would be set up throughout the lobby.

Now that we had a final schedule for the service, the slideshow, the video, and the performers, Dave arranged a final walk-through with the Long Center staff a few days before the service to make sure everything was ready to go. They also had the Green Room arranged with some refreshments for the family to meet an hour before the service began, along with a dressing room large enough for the performers to gather before they went on stage.

My family was arriving the day before the service, and I spent that morning going through the house getting all the bedrooms ready. Even though I was in a five-bedroom house, I didn't have room for everyone; one brother and his wife would be staying with friends in their downtown condo, and a sister would be staying with friends in South Austin. I brought in food to serve a luncheon for my family since they were all arriving on the same flight, but there was a slight delay at the rental car company. There had been a major hurricane in the Houston area the weekend before, and a lot of rental cars were being used to accommodate people's needs in that area, which severely limited the inventory in Austin. So when my family arrived at the airport, only one brother was able to get a vehicle, which happened to be a large pickup, and he had to go back to the airport to get everyone else who were stranded without cars. When they arrived at the house, it was reminiscent of the opening scene of the Beverly Hillbillies TV show because everyone was packed into the cab of the truck and their luggage was piled up and nearly overloaded but secured in the truck bed.

After lunch, some of them got settled in their rooms, and the rest of us gathered on the back porch, which in spite of the heat was comfortable due to large ceiling fans providing some relief. We hadn't been together in a long time because I had been unable to travel during the previous five years because I was taking care of James, and it was wonderful to see each other, despite the circumstances. In true Irish tradition, we began what was going to be a weekend-long event, an Irish wake. We broke out the beer and wine and began telling stories about James and our family. I was surprised that people were sharing stories about our family that I had never heard before, and this went on all weekend. We remained on the back porch for a few hours before we needed to get ready to go to dinner, where we would meet up with the friends who were taking some of my family members to stay in their homes.

Since we had never had had a full house, I recommended that some people shower that night and others do it in the morning to prevent us from running out of hot water. We had to be dressed and ready to go by 9:30 the next morning, when the funeral home had arranged for cars to pick us up and take us to the service. It was nice that we could arrange for the whole family to arrive at the same time, which was kind of a tradition for my family. For many years, whenever we were going to attend an event, whether it was a wedding, funeral, party, or reunion, we would gather somewhere first to have a drink, then go on to the event and walk in together. When we arrived at the Long Center, I showed them where the Green Room was and saw that a few people were already there. I was holding up well until I saw James' granddaughter, who had spent a lot of time with James and me over the years, and I lost it. This was the first time I had seen her since James' passing, so it was a very emotional moment. I later went to the dressing room to greet the artists and thank them for joining us; I got emotional again when I saw a few of the ZACH performers James and I had known for many years.

I was asked to join Dave on stage with the others who were going to speak to do a sound check. On my way back to the Green Room, I ran into some good friends, one of whom was a doctor, and I asked him about some medication I'd brought with me. Over the past weeks, whenever I had to talk about James, I would break down in tears and have difficulty carrying on a conversation. How would I hold up at the service? I mentioned this problem to a doctor-friend who recommended a medication she took whenever she had to speak to a large group. I got the prescription from my PCP but had never taken it before and wanted to make sure there would be no side effects if I took two pills prior to speaking at the service. My friend assured me it was fine.

I went back to the Green Room as it was getting close to the time to go into the auditorium, and I wanted to check in with my family to make sure they were ready. Everyone in the room was soon escorted through the back of the auditorium, where we could enter through a side door. Liz had asked to have all three sections of the front row reserved so she could direct where people could sit. My family sat in the second row in the center section, where I had easy access to go backstage when it was my turn to speak. While we were waiting for the service to begin, many of the guests came up to see me, that was a little difficult, but the medication seemed to be working. At one point, two of my brothers mentioned that they wanted to sit next to me so they could have my back if anyone gave me any grief, knowing how a couple of people had treated me in the past. Since these are the same two brothers who, until this day, are the only people I know who actually got kicked out of Gilley's, that popular honky-tonk outside of Houston that was featured in the film Urban Cowboy, I was a little concerned. I was appreciative of their support, but I asked them to make sure they didn't cause a scene in the auditorium. I eventually sat down and watched the slideshow. It was really well done, with excellent background music. A great beginning to what looked like it would be an exceptional memorial service that James would have loved.

The lights were dimmed in the auditorium. This was the first time I'd seen the stage illuminated to show the beautiful Ballet Austin scenery in the background. Spotlights shone on the lectern, on one side, and on the other side of the stage, with the painting of James and me from the opera gala, the beautiful flowers, and the box containing James' ashes with a Bentley model car on top. It was stunning—more beautiful than I could have ever imagined. I couldn't have been more proud and pleased that everyone's hard work had truly paid off. Dave came out to welcome everyone and began introducing the first performer. The program for the service read as follows:

The Memorial

Welcome Dave Steakley, ZACH Theatre Producing Artistic Director
    Performance by Zach Theatre: "The Glory of Love" and "I'll Be
    Seeing You"

Philip Barnes, Founding Board Member of Austin Opera
    Performance by Brett Barnes accompanied by Nyle Matsuoka

Peter Bay, Austin Symphony Music Director and Conductor
Performance by Mela Sarajane Dailey

Stephen Mills, Ballet Austin Artistic Director

Margaret Perry, Armstrong Community Music School Executive Director
Performance by Liz Cass

Doug Dempster, UT College of Fine Arts Dean
Performance by Invoke Quartet

Dr. Steven Hamilton

Brad Armstrong

Larry Connelly

Special Guest Speaker
Performance by ZACH Theatre: "Make Our Garden Grow" from
Candide and "One Hand, One Heart" from *West Side Story*

Everything was going so well; the flow of speaker followed by a performance was incredibly beautiful. This was the first time I had heard the different performances, and it seemed like it only got better as we progressed down the program. All of the speakers followed the guideline of staying within the three-minute time frame. The words they chose were very moving and highlighted many of James' incredible qualities. When James' longtime friend Dr. Steven Hamilton came out to speak, it was my cue to go backstage and wait my turn. A friend joined me backstage. I asked if he would mind being my wingman and if for any reason I couldn't finish my speech, he would step in and complete it for me. While I was waiting backstage, Pei San texted me with a concern about the mayor's arrival, uncertain whether he would make it before the service was over. She was in constant contact with the mayor's assistant, with a minute-by-minute update regarding where he was. Since we were aware that this might be a problem, we didn't include the mayor's name in the program, and I listed James' video as "Special Guest Speaker." This provided an opening for the mayor to be inserted in the lineup. I shared the updated information on the mayor's arrival with Dave, and he said he would make it work whenever the mayor arrived.

Once Dr. Hamilton was finished, Brad went on stage. He asked to not have a time limit, so I didn't know how long he planned to speak. In the end, this actually worked out for us because as Brad was speaking, the mayor arrived backstage at a perfect time to go on stage once Brad was finished. This also allowed me a few moments to say hello to the mayor and his wife; we hadn't seen each other since James had passed away. I don't know how long Brad spoke, but eventually, he finished, and Dave went out to introduce the mayor, who did an excellent job of speaking about James and all he had done for the city of Austin. He stressed that James' contributions were deeply appreciated by the city, making it a much better place to call home. It created a wonderful moment for me to make my entrance and share my thoughts about James and our life together. My speech read as follows:

> I'd like to begin with a few words of thanks to some people who helped make all of this happen. First would be Ballet Austin, who provided us with the Long Center on your opening night for Romeo and Juliet. We especially would like to thank Pei San Brown, who did a LOT of the coordination.
>
> Then there is Darrell May (along with Michael and Sergio), who all helped to create the wonderful slideshow. David Kurio and Michael O'Krent played crucial roles, and we truly want to thank the various speakers and performers who helped make this celebration so special. And to the Shores, who let us display this wonderful painting of James. And lastly, Dave Steakley and the ZACH staff, who stepped up to make this so special and professional and at a high quality level James deserves.
>
> It is so fitting that there is a car show next door at the Palmer. I'm sure James has been struggling all morning as to where to

place his focus because he LOVED car shows, and I know he's had an eye on it this morning. That's why I'd like to thank Sonny Morgan at Austin Bentley, who helped me secure this beautiful Bentley model that I'm sure James is focused on, and he can use it to drive to his glory in the fashion to which he had become accustomed.

It's still hard to believe that a chance meeting in Houston thirty-three years ago would turn into such an amazing, incredible, happy, and loving relationship because we were leading such different lives at the time. He was a social icon in high-Houston society (though I didn't find that out for months into the relationship), and I was a small-town farm boy who was teaching school in the 5th Ward and working as a waiter at night. My first inkling of how special he was happened when one of my roommates said he needed to have a talk with me. He said he noticed that I had not been spending as much time at the house as I usually did and asked if I had met someone and who was it. I said I had, and his name was James Armstrong. My roommate sat back and had the strangest look on his face and asked, THE James Armstrong? It was many months later, after traveling with him or attending many parties and galas that I found out why he was referred to as THE James Armstrong.

But for me, he was someone else. He was so kind and protective and, in the fall, slowly introduced me into his world. And it was a huge leap for me. But one day, after so many amazing parties and galas, he asked me to stop standing behind him and said he wanted me to stand next to him as an equal. At that point, he went from being THE James Armstrong to someone I called MY FAVORITE HONEY.

Shortly after that, we moved here to Austin, where our relationship took a new turn. The people here were so warm, welcoming, and inclusive, and we quickly became referred to as "James and Larry," and standing next to him was not a problem. Because of the way we were treated so positively, it was easy for us to want to give back to the community. He did it with some major gifts to capital campaigns, endowments, annual gifts, etc., and I joined various boards and committees and chaired a few galas.

Now many people, through e-mails, cards, and Facebook posts, have said we need to find a way to keep the legacy James created alive. And I think I have found a way to do this with your help. James loved telling stories and especially loved hearing stories about him. Well, if you've had many interactions with him, then you have a story to tell … about something that happened or something he said or did.

I think by sharing these stories with each other, we will keep his amazing legacy alive. Now to jog your memories, I am providing a few examples that are kind of some of his life's lessons.

The first, which I can't believe I am sharing and wouldn't except for the fact at least five or six people have already shared this one with me over the past few weeks. James always said, as you get older, there are two things to remember; never pass up a bathroom and NEVER trust a fart.

Now the next one is something he frequently said in his Houston days, and that is, "You can never have the same good time twice." I took this as a personal goal to try and break this rule, and I think we came really close on his eightieth birthday. We were having a party at the house for family and out-of-town guests, and we needed some entertainment. Our dear friend

Bobbi said there's only one person and it's the cabaret singer who performed on his fiftieth birthday because he still talks about her. But when I questioned if she was still performing after thirty years, it was all Bobbi needed, and by the next day, Marilyn Maye was located, and she was still performing, mostly in New York, but she agreed to come to Austin and perform in our home. What was even more amazing is that we were able to keep this a secret from James until I announced her name at the dinner, and he was so happy and had a wonderful time … the same good time twice.

The last one is from his near and dear friend, the great Beverly Sills. She frequently said, and he repeated, "I don't share credit, and I don't share the blame. And I most certainly don't share my dessert." I can't count the number of times I witnessed this at various meals, and he would always say, if you want some of my dessert, I'll be happy to get one for you. But after many years, at least twenty, I was able to get my fork to his plate and taste his dessert without resistance.

So now it is up to you to help keep his remarkable legacy alive. As you travel around Austin, you will see James' name. Whether it is at the Thinkery Children's Museum at the Mueller site, or taking a class in the studio at Ballet Austin that bears our names, or here at the Long Center in the Grand Staircase. You will also see his name at the top of a program for an Austin Symphony children's concert. And maybe you are taking a class or attending a recital at the Armstrong Community Music School, or attending a performance at ZACH, where his name is all over the Topfer Theatre. Well, when you see his name, take a minute to remember a story about James and share it with the people around you. If enough people do this, we will then accomplish the goal of keeping James' legacy alive. Thank you.

And now a few words from a very special guest. The person who changed my life forever and I referred to for so many years as "My Favorite Honey."

The video played next; it was very well done. It was a wonderful way to remember James because it was all in his words. It was also an opportunity for people to see and hear James one more time. Since he left us so quickly, no one had had the opportunity to say goodbye.

The following week the newspaper published an article about James' Celebration of Life ceremony. I'm not sure I've ever seen a write-up about a memorial service in a newspaper before. I thought it was well done and share it with you here:

Hats off to the James Armstrong Celebration of Life

Artists know how to celebrate even in mourning. A tribute to major benefactor James Armstrong was every bit as compelling as a show staged by one of the outstanding arts groups represented on stage of the Long Center for the Performing Arts.

First, the flowers, which were everywhere and overwhelmingly beautiful. Then the crowd, which included Armstrong's husband, Larry Connelly, and his family, as well as hundreds of respectful admirers.

One after another Dave Steakley (Zach Theatre), Philip Barnes (Austin Lyric Opera), Peter Bay (Austin Symphony), Stephen Mills (Ballet Austin), Margaret Perry (Armstrong Community Music School), Doug Dempster (University of Texas College of Fine Arts) and others talked of Armstrong's generosity, humor and ardency for life.

Almost every speech came with a performance of a song or aria or medley. Each was extraordinary, but I was taken unawares by Liz Cass' deep, rich, heartfelt rendition of "Mon Coeur s'ouvre a ta voix" from Camille Saint-Saens's "Samson and Delilah." You never know what will make you choke back tears.

Life well lived, James!

Reprinted with permission
Austin American Statesman
Thursday, September 21, 2017
Michael Barnes, p. D8

After the service, we met with a lot of the guests. This was the first time I had seen many of them since James' passing, so it was very emotional. After a few hours, I gathered my family together, and we left to return to Scenic. We eventually ended up on the back porch again and talked about the service, sharing more stories about James and his involvement with our family. A few friends stopped by who knew some of my siblings and wanted to spend more time visiting with them. Before long, it was time to get ready to go to dinner before attending the ballet performance honoring James. When we arrived at the performing arts center, we were escorted to a box on one side of the auditorium; some of the Armstrong family members were in a box across the hall. Soon the lights dimmed, and the usual short video about Ballet Austin was shown. What I didn't expect was that when the video ended, there was a screened message stating that this performance was dedicated to James. The audience erupted into applause, which was very moving.

I think this was the first ballet performance my family had ever attended, and they enjoyed it. It helped that they were very familiar with the Romeo and Juliet story. After the performance, we went straight home. It had been a long day, and everyone was ready for bed. The next morning, it took some time for everyone to make their way to the kitchen for tea or coffee and onto the back porch for pastry. I made reservations for lunch at a nearby restaurant on the lake, where we were surprised to run into James' granddaughter and her boyfriend, who, like us, were taking an emotional break from the previous day's activities. When we returned home, some took a well-deserved nap while the rest of us gathered on the back porch to continue our Irish wake and visit with friends who stopped by. This continued into the evening when we went in for a farewell dinner of salad and pizza as everyone would be leaving the next day. It was so nice to have all of the family gathered together again. I received many comments from friends who complimented me on how well we got along. They could tell we were very close and deeply committed to each other, which was not the case for so many families. I felt very lucky.

But after they left, I was alone again, and it was taking a toll on me. I still had trouble talking about James without becoming emotional and tearing up. For the first time in my life, I understood how people get so depressed that they would consider suicide. Over the next few weeks, I was invited to dinner by a number of friends, and at some point during the dinner, they would bring up my state of mind and offer suggestions about getting to a better place in my life. A turning point for me was when I had to attend a luncheon where James and I were being honored for our support for a local non-profit. This had been in the planning stages for months. When James passed, I offered them the opportunity to choose someone else for the honor, but they declined.

I knew attending this luncheon was going to be difficult for me. When I was contacted by the organization to talk about the details of the event, I was asked if I would like to invite anyone as my guest. I replied that I would like to have a couple join me for support, and she happily agreed. I didn't realize this would cause a problem until I received an email from Patti, the estate administrator. She stated that I had a "list" of people invited to the luncheon, and she was concerned about having too many people at the tables she had purchased.

Not wanting to cause any problems, I replied with the following and copied Lauren, who was my contact person for the luncheon:

> I guess you need to speak with Lauren as she said I could invite two guests. If it's a problem, we can sit with someone else.
>
> Larry

Patti now didn't seem concerned with my "list" and said it wasn't a problem; she wanted me to have friends join me. I still didn't want to have any issues at the luncheon and sent the following, which I again copied to Lauren:

> Patti
>
> It's OK. I will have Lauren find other arrangements for my two friends and me and I am willing to buy three tickets for the event, if need be. We don't want to impose on your financial commitments or your potential guest lists and commitments.
>
> Larry

Patti replied that she just needed to know the names of who was being invited. It would not be a problem for us to sit at one of her tables, and she would love to have us. I replied with thanks for including us at her tables and was glad to get this behind me.

On the day of the luncheon, I picked up my two guests so we could arrive together. For some reason, I was feeling very anxious. When we arrived at the event, I was sweating, and my hands were cold. I'm not sure why I was reacting this way and regretted not taking any of my anxiety pills from the day of the memorial. Fortunately, I did not have to make a speech, as we had stipulated when we were asked to be honored, that we would accept if we didn't have to talk. Patti volunteered to say something on our behalf. As I waited off-stage for Patti to finish speaking, I still was not feeling well and could not stop pacing back and forth.

The time finally came for me to go on stage and receive the award. I was blinded by the spotlight on the lectern and was caught off guard by a thunderous roar of applause and a standing ovation from the audience. This is when I completely lost it and broke down in tears; still, the applause went on. When they finally stopped, I could only say a few words of thanks for the honor and how I appreciated the support of the audience for this non-profit and the wonderful work they did. I went back to my seat but could not eat anything. I just wanted to leave, but I knew I would have to stay for the duration of the event. The director of the organization approached me after the luncheon. She wanted to thank me for my participation in their fundraiser. Her husband, however, said how concerned he was about me and said if I needed to talk with someone for emotional support, he had a few references he would be happy to share with me.

I shared this experience with my two guests as we drove home, and they agreed that I was in bad shape. They said one thing that could help me would be to get out of the house, find a place of my own, and begin a new life. Their suggestion was to find a place downtown, where they lived. They said it would be good for me as I would be around people every day. For me to start feeling better, I needed to leave Scenic, where I had so many memories of James and where I was too isolated. I knew they were right, but I wasn't sure I was ready to go through that much change so soon after James' death.

I shared this idea with a number of friends. They were all in agreement and said they would do anything to help. A few days later, I was invited to an event downtown hosted by a couple of friends. I was one of the first to arrive, so I had ample time to talk with the hosts and mentioned this idea of moving downtown. Both of them had lived downtown at some point and agreed it would do me good to make a move.

I guess they really thought this was a good idea because the next day, they sent an e-mail to a real estate agent we all knew, who had been at the event the previous night and copied me. The message asked the agent to work with me to locate a new downtown residence. The agent called me the next day, and we made an appointment to meet for lunch to discuss what I might be interested in seeing. During lunch, we narrowed down the search to a specific section of downtown, made the decision to lease rather than purchase, and created two lists of potential buildings. One list was of condos for lease, and the other list was selected apartment buildings in the designated area. Over the next few weeks, the agent sent me a variety of options for me to review and identify units I was interested in seeing.

While this apartment search was going on I received the following e-mail from Brad:

9/27/17

Hi Larry,

Dad's memorial service was amazing, wondrous. All the effort and time put into it produced such a beautiful tribute.

I'm following up about a few things.

1. First of all, we need to get Dad's ashes from the funeral home. We could keep them at Scenic or elsewhere until we bury them (or at least the bulk of them) in Ft. Worth on Dad's birthday. Would you also like some of Dad's ashes for yourself? Let me know your thoughts.

2. We're wondering if there might be notes of condolence from family or friends that came to Scenic for us. We'd like to respond to these. Please pass them to Jennifer.

3. We would also like to arrange some time when we are in Austin over the next 6 months (I'll probably be there 4–5 times; Liz about the same) to come to Scenic and begin going through some of Dad's personal items (photos, books) that we'd like to have as mementos.

Hope you're well and recovering from the shock of losing Dad.

Best,
Brad

Though I appreciated the improved tone of this e-mail, I was a little uncomfortable about having to see Brad, not knowing when he might turn on me, and especially having him in the house with me. I asked my lawyer for advice, and he recommended going through everything first, pre-sorting the items that were mine, and placing them in a secure area. He reminded me that per the marital property agreement, I was entitled to the library books of my choosing. He closed by saying that the bottom line was I should designate the area Brad would have access to.

Then I got the following e-mail from Liz:

9/29/17

Hi Larry,

Thanks for the info you sent in Brad's email. As he mentioned, I will be in town next week for a couple of days. I am hoping your schedule will allow me to come by the house for a couple of hours on Thursday, Oct 5th, from 11:30–2.

I would like to start to put a dent in going through photos and Dad's record albums.

I'll also be back at the end of the month on Oct 31 and Nov 1. Perhaps we can schedule times that are convenient for you on those days when I am there next week.

Hugs, liz

Boy, she sure can be nice when she wants something. I had about a week to go through everything before she arrived. It would easily take that long, as James and I kept everything, and there was a lot to go through.

As if this wasn't enough to deal with, I began getting e-mails from the administrators that were related to the estate. The first e-mails were about the leased Mercedes I drove as my day-to-day car. Though the lease still had five months before it expired, they, for some reason, wanted to return it to the dealership within the next two weeks. This would leave me with the

Flex, which was part of the marital agreement. They sent me the contact information for the dealership, and I started getting the car prepared for the upcoming pick-up day. A few weeks later, after the car had been picked up, the owner of the Mercedes dealership, who lived in the neighborhood, was driving by and stopped to say hello to me. He asked me where my Mercedes was, and I told him about the dealership picking it up. He questioned this, as it was still under lease, and he seemed certain that they would not have forgiven the remainder of the lease payments. He appeared a little upset that they had done this to me and asked who he needed to call or if there was anything he could do to remedy the situation. I thanked him for his concern but said it was likely a done deal, and I doubted he could get the car back for me. He just shook his head in disbelief and went on his way.

The other set of e-mails addressed appraisals and estate valuation. They had selected an appraiser and were looking at three dates two weeks hence, asking if these days would be convenient for me to allow entry into my residence. I responded that the days were fine, except that I had an appointment on the first day, and they would need to leave by 1:30. I also asked what times they were going to be there on the other days.

Jennifer replied that leaving early on the first day would not work; they would need full-day access to the house on all three days. Also, it would be impossible to provide a time frame before seeing the contents of the house. I then asked why they even asked me if this schedule would work for me if this were the way it was going to happen, and my convenience was not a consideration? All she could say was that it was explained to her after she sent the initial e-mail.

When the day of the appraisal arrived, I was feeling a little uncomfortable. The appraiser arrived with four other people to begin going through the house. It just didn't feel right having a group of strangers going through everything. Also, I didn't appreciate the way this intrusion was handled. It didn't help that Patti and Jennifer showed up and sat in the middle of the living room to oversee the process. They acted like they were at a tea party, laughing and carrying on but really not making any useful contributions. The appraiser was working off of a copy of a thorough appraisal we had done about ten years earlier that detailed all of the furniture, antiques, art, and other valuables, including photos, so I wasn't sure why Patti and Jennifer thought they needed to be there. I decided to stay out of the way and went down to my office to work. But I was frequently interrupted with questions from the appraiser because Patti and Jennifer could offer no assistance. I don't know if the appraiser said something or they figured it out themselves, but Patti and Jennifer did not return on the following days of the appraisal process.

The appraisal was finally finished by the end of the week. I expressed my concern when I saw that they had included some furniture and other pieces that were mine in the estate appraisal. But they didn't think it would affect my marital agreement and soon left. I received a few follow-up inquiries, but it seemed like this process was complete.

Meanwhile, Brad and Liz continued to come by the house on a nearly monthly basis, and though Brad was being respectful of my privacy and followed the guidelines set by their lawyer, Liz would do what she typically did—pushing the envelope and finding ways to step over the boundaries. One example comes from the following e-mail from Liz:

> Hi Larry,
>
> I'll be back in Austin next week. I'd like to come by the house on Wed Nov 1st from 1:30–3:30. Will you be around to let me in or shall I get the key and let myself in?
>
> Liz

Seriously, "get the key and let myself in?" She knew that no one was supposed to enter the house without me being present, and she was going to attempt to go beyond what was allowed. If I had agreed to this, I would have opened the door for her to enter the house whenever it suited her. I said I would be at the house when she arrived. The next e-mail illustrates another overreach of asking to take things from the house while I was still living there. Liz wrote:

Hi Larry,

I will be visiting Austin again in mid December. I'll be there both Monday, Dec 18th and tuesday, Dec 19th. Brad is likely to be there as well. Would it work for us to come to the house on Monday afternoon from 4–6 and on Tuesday from 10:30–2:30?

I also have a sensitive question to pose to you. Dad's wishes are that all his bedding and clothing go to you. Might you consider passing the gold monogrammed napping blanket that Patti and Jennifer gave dad to Brandi? Might you also consider sharing a couple of Dad's beloved hats with Tobiah and Adrien? (specifically the Olympic and the Bentley hats) We respect any answer you come to. Simply a request as it would mean so much to Dad's grandchildren to have a special part of him.

Wishing you a nice Thanksgiving.
liz

Of course I agreed to this request. I sent the blanket to Brandi, and Liz collected the hats on her next visit. But then she also took James' model car collection, and I'm not sure what else she might have taken. On this visit, I thought it was kind of strange that they asked me if I planned to stay in the house until it sold or if I had plans to move out before then. I'm not sure if they found out I was in search of an apartment downtown or if they had another purpose and replied I hadn't yet made a decision. Liz also brought up that Brad's wife was interested in one of the art pieces, but I said I wouldn't make the decision as to which six pieces I was going to take until I had found a place to live and could see what would best fit in my new place. Brad said he wasn't going to say anything to his wife until after I moved out, and I was happy to have this conversation end. But leave it to Liz to take another step outside the boundary with the following e-mail:

Thanks Larry. I'm glad you like the plan.

We're beginning to make plans with the art. You mentioned that you know what your six art pieces are. Would you please share those so we all know what is off the table? It would be very helpful.

Hoping you have a peaceful holiday.

I should have known that with every visit to the house, Liz would try to go outside the established guidelines and keep pushing with no regard to decency and respect of others. I responded with the following:

I thought we talked about this when you were last here. The list your dad and I made is longer than 6 pieces and I said I was waiting for a final decision on which 6 pieces after I know where I'll be living and how much space I have. I really don't like being pressured to make decisions before I am ready. I had to go through this with Patti and Jennifer already when they came over and wanted me to make decisions about furniture before I was ready and it was very uncomfortable. All of this is still very difficult for me and I don't need any added pressure … I feel bad enough about making these decisions as it is. And in any case, nothing is supposed to be removed until after I leave anyway so I'm not sure what plans you are making and I don't need to know.

I think in the future, we will follow your lawyer's suggestion that any future communication (questions, inquiries, etc.) go though him to my lawyer and I stay out of the loop until I move and I will relay all final decisions through my lawyer to your lawyer as they occur. So I will not be responding to future e-mails. I just need to be left alone at this time.

I hope you can understand my feelings in all of this.

Larry

But needing to have the last word she came back with:

Dear Larry,

I do hope you read this. I am truly sorry if this made you feel any sort of pressure. I did not intend that what so ever. This is a hard process for everyone, not just you. But it is a process that must be done regardless. It is also what Dad would want. He was never one to linger.

I must have misunderstood our conversation at the house about the art. When we talked about it you said you and Dad had chosen six pieces and that you would be honoring his wishes. Since you didn't elaborate more than that your comment simply led me to believe that you already knew your choices. That is all. If you do not know yet then we will wait.

I am sorry you feel the need to pull away from us. I do understand the difficult time of mourning. We are all deeply wounded at Dad's passing. There is certainly the option of coming together as much as there is to pull apart.

See you in 2018.

liz

I noticed she copied Brad on this e-mail, though I am not sure why since my response was directed to her only, and these last few e-mails were only between the two of us. I didn't respond to her and was happy that she seemed to have gotten the message; I didn't hear from her again.

During all of this, my realtor and I continued to visit various downtown residences. We were nearing the end of our list when we toured a fairly new building where I had once visited some friends who were living there and looked at a couple of the models. But it wasn't until we looked at the last apartment that I thought I had found exactly what I was looking for in a new home. I told my agent that I wanted to enjoy this view for a few minutes before he asked the manager what it would cost because I was sure it was over my budget. After he talked to the manager, he told me the cost, and I thought there was no way my investment manager would approve. But when I called him and described the apartment and that I would be the first occupant, he said he wanted to come over to check it out. We met the following day, and once he saw the space, he said he understood what I liked about it and agreed that I could get it. My realtor and I met with the apartment agent to work out the details of the lease and agreed on a move-in date about six weeks away.

During this time of transition, I was still working through my lawyer to finish any business related to James' estate. One of the lingering issues involved the transfer of credit card rewards points to me. One of the cards was in both of our names, so those points just remained on my card. But the other card was in James' name alone, and it became an issue as to whom they belonged. When I called the credit card company to use points to fly home for the holidays, I asked what the policy was for transferring the points when the cardholder passed away. I was told they could only be transferred to a surviving spouse; otherwise, they became invalid. But when I pursued this action, I found out the points had already been redeemed for cash and no longer existed. Through further investigation, I found out the estate administrators had counted the points as an estate asset. Though I don't know how they were able to do this, I thought it was a done deal and out of my hands.

Another issue was about a long-term health-care policy James had purchased for me and for two of his children that were titled in the name of James' Management Trust. This was most likely done to avoid a taxable gift at the time they were purchased. It was thought that the policies would transfer over to us at the time of James' death, but some people involved with the estate felt differently. They thought these policies were part of the estate and that I would need to purchase mine if I wanted to keep it. When a friend of ours found out about this, who was also one of our investment managers and the one who sold these policies to James, he sent the following e-mail to my lawyer:

> Here is the most recent statement for the policy for Larry. There is no doubt that James's intent in buying this was for Brad, Tony and Larry to have long term care for the rest of their life. Not for any of them to have to purchase it back at his death if that makes any difference. If he had known this would be the result, it is my opinion that he would not have purchased it in the Trust but rather in each of their names.
>
> We need to keep it for Larry so if the end result is purchasing it, then we need to do it. But I would view that as really playing hardball with Larry rather than doing what is right based on James intentions. I have made that clear to Patti and Jennifer in an email. I was the financial advisor that discussed this with James and convinced him he should do this for each child and Larry. Patti and Jennifer were involved in those conversations. Otherwise none of them would have this major benefit. Lincoln has a form that Brad will have to sign in either case. Nora will go ahead and get the form from them.
>
> Let me know if you need to discuss further. We are trying to get the policy, but if they don't send it to us it will require Larry to call and request. I think this is probably all you need.

Over the next few months, my lawyer continued communicating with their lawyer over these two issues. At one point, my lawyer said if the estate would not treat the healthcare policy as a gift, then we should pursue the issue of the transfer of the credit card points to me. He also wanted to make sure that, unlike the healthcare policy, they would not be deducted from my inheritance since the transfer would be done by the credit card account agreement. I agreed with him that this was the route I would like to take. With all of these estate-related issues surfacing, it seemed like a "Mean Team" was being formed consisting of Brad, Liz, Patti, and Jennifer. Their actions with the settling of the estate were so far removed from James' intention and what he would have wanted. It was so sad that over all these years, they had not learned from James' generous and thoughtful way of treating others and were not doing a very good job of honoring James' intentions. At one point, my lawyer asked me if I was aware of how much I was leaving on the table since there is precedent in Texas law related to same-sex couples recognizing common-law marriages and inheritance. I said I was aware but felt it was important to honor James' wishes and follow the Marital Trust as it was stated in his will.

As my moving date got closer, it appeared that we were coming to an end in settling the estate. My lawyer shared some information he received from their lawyer about transferring the long-term health care policy to me. He thought their lawyer might have heard something about my plans to move because he reiterated that I was welcome to remain at Scenic until it sold. But if I planned to move out earlier, he needed to prepare bill-of-sale documents to show the transfer of items James had given to me. My lawyer then suggested to me that I not take anything out of the house until we received the bills of sale since the items given to me were technically part of the estate.

Their lawyer also said he understood that I had requested all communication go through my lawyer to him. My lawyer corrected him, saying that I had no issues with Brad. Their lawyer agreed that Liz could be difficult and said he would pass this information on to Brad. It is interesting how the truth finds a way to come out in the end.

After we discussed this, my lawyer contacted theirs to let him know I would begin moving out on February 1 and take a week to complete the move. He also took one more shot and brought up how it was understood by some that the healthcare policy would pass on to me automatically and expressed his opinion that this would be the normal process. Their lawyer just said that he would continue working on the bills of sale and the transfer of the long-term care policy to me.

Some people seemed to have problems understanding "take a week to complete the move." On February 2, their lawyer contacted mine, saying he'd been told that I had completely moved out of Scenic. Also, the estate administrators needed some information from me to terminate certain services such as IDs, security questions, and passwords for the telephone, security, and cable services. They also accused me of having taken the cable boxes with me and said that I needed to return them and get my own cable equipment in my name. What idiots! How did they not know that when you contact the cable company to install a new service, they tell you NOT to take the current boxes with you to your new home? I knew the cable company would be delivering new equipment for my apartment. They gave me instructions on what needed to be turned in and where the nearest drop-off location was. When I began disconnecting the TVs I would be taking with me, I put all of the cable equipment into a box and turned it into the cable company that morning, and had the receipt delivered to the administrators.

That evening my lawyer responded to their lawyer, telling him I was not completely moved out and to correct whoever was saying I was gone. He also said how frustrated he was since even though he provided specific move-out dates, someone declared me gone days ahead of the stated date. He also confirmed that we would provide the requested information to terminate some of the Scenic services. But like me, he wondered why they would need this information to terminate services. A few days later, my lawyer requested that the administrators hold off on canceling any utilities or re-keying the property since the bill of sale would not be completed until the 21st.

On the 20th, I received a preliminary draft of the new appraisal with items circled that they thought I had taken and wanted me to confirm its accuracy. They also agreed to sign a mutual release form created by

my lawyer stating that the estate had no claim to property in my possession. They didn't agree to have the health-care policy roll over to me, so
its value was deducted from my inheritance. But I did receive in cash the
value of James' rewards points from his credit card. A few days later, I
went over to my lawyer's office to sign the mutual release paperwork and
receive the final bill of sale. When it was over, my lawyer commented
that after working together all these months, this was the first time he
had seen me smile. I just replied that it was finally over and I would
never have to work with the Mean Team again, which made me very
happy and relieved. But I was happy to have my wonderful memories of
my life with James and continue my positive relationships with James'
grandchildren and his younger son, who I referred to as "the nice one."

Should you wish to help keep James' legacy alive, please consider a
donation in James' memory to one of his most supported non-profits
where I am still involved to this day. Zach Theatre or Armstrong Community Music School located in Austin, Texas.

EPILOGUE

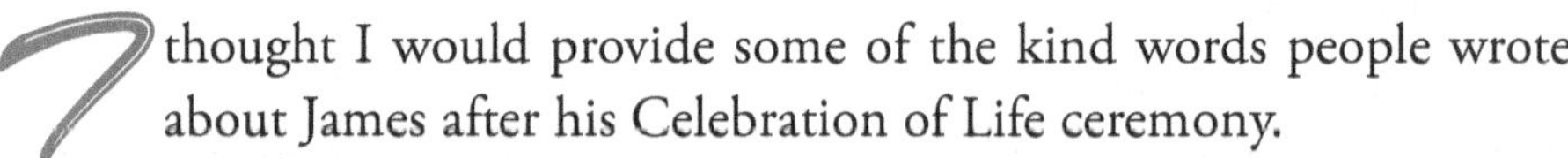

I thought I would provide some of the kind words people wrote about James after his Celebration of Life ceremony.

In Loving Memory

We are deeply saddened to have lost James Armstrong, the wonderful man our school is named for. His caring spirit and generosity set a standard. His philanthropic work touched many lives in our community and he has left a lasting legacy. We will always be proud our school bears his name.

Armstrong Community Music School

Remembering James Armstrong … RIP, Good Man

In retrospect, the Gods and Larry conspired nicely to enable one last visit. Two weeks ago at the opening of Million Dollar Quartet at ZACH, a favorite charitable beneficiary of James' and Larry's generosity. I sit near them at ZACH, and Larry asked if I would sit with James for a few minutes. James had a strategic wheelchair seating slot, and I eagerly joined him. Now, I realize the blessing of that synchronicity.

James lived next to my parents in Midland before he moved to Austin. He and I always enjoyed our visits, and this one was especially interesting. We reflected on West Texas characters such as Roy Orbison and Buddy Holly (in the context of the show we were enjoying). And we talked again about the flamboyant Midland cateress Janice Constantine, for whom James drove his Rolls Royce for her showbiz grand entry to the World Chili Cookoff in Terlingua. James had on his full driver's regalia and members of the Midland/Odessa Symphony accompanied them in the desert dirt.

James was a gentleman, a gentle man, a generous philanthropist, an interested and active arts enthusiast, a friend to many and a wonderful partner to Larry. Larry has been a devoted saint in recent years as James' health was in decline. I wish Blessings and Grace on James and his family and with Larry as he experiences this life transition. James Armstrong has left a tremendous legacy of good works. Larry Connelly is a worthy steward of that legacy. Our community is the better for both of them …

Dan

We were so saddened to hear this news. We send our sincerest condolences to Larry, and to James' family. He was a dear man of grace, generosity, and humor, and left a wonderful legacy. It was a life well lived. We will sorely miss him.

Marcy & John

It is with sadness that I recently learned of the death of James, a friend of 30 years. His style and generosity I will always remember. Condolences to Larry, his children, and the rest of the family at this sad time.

Anonymous

Larry, thinking of you during this difficult time. James was such a kind and giving man. He was a blessing to so many people! He will be dearly missed.

Pete & Misti

James leaves a legacy of generosity and friendship, and he surely ranks among our heroes in his support for the arts and the greater Austin community. He will be greatly missed and always remembered.

Robert

The Austin arts scene will never be the same with the loss of James Armstrong. His influence and generosity will live on in the institutions that he supported. What a fine man he was. We send our condolences. He is missed.

Forrest & Linda

How fitting that the memorial service is to be at the Joe R. and Teresa Long Center for the Performing Arts. This center is where so many children have had their first experience with great music over the years, thanks to James. His strong and steady generosity in enriching each new generation with musical greatness is a gift beyond price. Musicians thrive on the feedback of enthusiastic audiences and patrons. Bravo, Larry, for extending his life for many worthy years.

Nancy

James was such a contribution to Austin, and he will be missed for the many ways he contributed and participated in the many music and arts events and happenings here! Such a wonderfully kind, eloquent and sharp witted, generous, and sweet man … Sending much love and big hugs to Larry at this time.

Kimberly

He was such a dear man and I know you will miss him. I was always so touched by his warmth and generosity. He will be missed, but certainly never forgotten.

Carol

How lucky Austin was to have had such a wonderful, involved, and generous citizen for so many years. I can only imagine how difficult it is for you.

Lew

James will always be remembered as the fun-loving, kind, and generous soul he was. I will never forget driving him on several occasions to our monthly lunch when he shared with me the wisdom of his life lessons. I am so glad that before coming to Santa Fe, I got to have one last dinner with the two of you together. All who knew James are experiencing a great loss, and you have my deepest sympathy.

Robin

James was a wonderful human being who was loved by many and will always be remembered for his generous contributions to the arts and special programs and his kindness to all. James' gift to ASO Education was a dream come true for me and thousands of children in Austin. Because of him, the programs will continue and will be a living legacy in his honor. A blessing indeed!

Diana

What an inspiration the two of you have been to our community, but to me personally as a young philanthropist working in the arts. Thank you for the legacy you have helped him build for so many to benefit.

Jennifer

It was such an honor to have known James, a remarkable man. His spirit of kindness and generosity will live through those who loved him.

Andrea & Jack

James was a gentleman and a gentle man. I recall one concert in Austin where the musicians were Jr High School age. It was one of the activities he had sponsored. Without fanfare, he slipped into the auditorium after the lights were down, then left before the final note was played. He didn't want any attention, but he paid attention to the activities he supported. When we first became involved w/ the opera, James gave us some good advice along that line. And, we listened. We will miss the care he showed for others, his generosity as a host, that smile that lit up his face … and the two of you, walking in to a room.

Suzanne & John

James was a kind and generous soul; a gentleman who was loved and respected by many in Austin and beyond. He will be missed.

Karen & Gene

We were blessed, as were so many, by our friendship with James. The article in the paper was a wonderful tribute to his "Life & Time." A gentleman in every respect. The memories we have will be cherished. It was truly an honor to have shared time together. His passion and dedication to so many things will continue to benefit many.

Vernon & Buddy

He—more than anyone—imbued hope for artists here in Austin. His belief in my work was a great honor that continues to inspire me daily. He made the world a better place and you gave him the joy that helped him accomplish all that he did.

Mary & Carl

His strength of character and huge heart will forever be a shining example for me, and for so many.

Laura

James was our favorite human, he was as mischievous and witty as he was insightful and kind. We all know James Armstrong's life and contributions were vast, rich, and deep, that he traveled and supported causes all over the world, but the best of James was in his heart, in his eyes and his gentle laugh. They were James' best gift to us.

We'll always remember you, James.

Love,

Mary & Rusty

You and James epitomized what is so good about Austin … your generosity of both spirit and purse, your steadfast humor and resolve, your friendship and mentoring to so many in the arts, and your love and devotion to each other. To say that Austin is a better place because of James is such an understatement that it feels almost trite to say it. The contributions he made to Austin will benefit generations for years to come and he could not have chosen a better life partner to live out his legacy.

Becky

www.ingramcontent.com/pod-product-compliance
Lightning Source LLC
Chambersburg PA
CBHW060540160726

47991CB00001B/407